THE DOG AND THE GUN

THE DOG AND THE GUN

Crawford Little

Lochar Publishing • Moffat • Scotland

Published by Lochar Publishing Ltd
MOFFAT DG10 9ED

British Library Cataloguing in Publication Data
Little, Crawford
  The dog and the gun.
  1. Gun dogs
  I. Title
  636.752

ISBN 0-948403-50-0

Typeset in 10pt Goudy Old Style by BEECEE Typesetting Services

Printed in Great Britain by BPCC Wheatons Ltd, Exeter

Contents

CHAPTER ONE   *My Shooting Companions*   9

CHAPTER TWO   *Two Centuries of Gundogs*   29

CHAPTER THREE   *Dogs on the Formal Shoot*   49

CHAPTER FOUR   *Snipe and Woodcock*   71

CHAPTER FIVE   *Rough Shooting*   93

CHAPTER SIX   *Grouse*   109

CHAPTER SEVEN   *Duck and Geese*   127

CHAPTER EIGHT   *Thoughts on Training*   141

CHAPTER NINE   *Random Shots*   155

One man and his dog — away from the formal scene.

Introduction

ONE OF THE STRANGE THINGS ABOUT A BOOK IS THAT THE INTRO-duction, which appears at the start, is written at the end. There is a good reason. No writer can introduce a book to the reader until they know what manner of beast they have produced. Another convention of the in-troduction to a book, in the modern age at least, is that it normally contains an apology. So why another book on gundogs because, surely, the subject has already been covered in exhaustive detail?

I only mention these things because they seem to serve as an introduction to my own thoughts on gundogs, and the words that have been written about them. Most books and magazine articles have gone into great detail about the various stages of training a puppy through to the day when it is ready to take its place in the shooting field. To a shooting man, like myself, while not seeking to criticise, this might seem rather like writing the introduction, but then failing to produce the book. Training is fundamental, and we must build on strong foundations, but we should never forget that it is nothing more than a means to an end. And that end is a faithful and useful shooting companion who will raise to an altogether higher plane our enjoyment of treasured days spent on moor, marsh and shore, or among the more intimate scenery of fields, hedgerows and coverts.

If this book serves as a reminder to some of what gundogs are all about, then I will feel that the writing of it has been worthwhile. It has been written against the backdrop of the closing decade of a century where we may have drifted towards an attitude that the training and handling of dogs is no longer a role for those who do the shooting. Letters are written to the sporting press which suggest that shoots could be run far more efficiently if the dog work was left to the keepers, pickers-up and the beaters. Well, perhaps they would, but how do we equate efficiency with enjoyment?

Professional and semi-professional trainers have taken a firm grip on the lead of who says what about gundogs. In terms of training, this is very right and proper, and it is why I have very largely refrained from saying more than a few words on the subject. But going back to the means to an end, how far can the professional trainer look beyond an open cheque book? Again, this is not so much a criticism as an observation. The life of a professional trainer is at best still precarious. They may have little time or perhaps inclination to make an individual dog into a personal shooting companion, rather than a sporting servant. If they see an end in the shooting field, it is likely to be no further than in picking-up as experience for field trials.

As described in this book, I have had a gundog or dogs of various types virtually as long as I have owned a gun. Without them, my shooting days and life in general would have been a far poorer experience. None of them would have won a field trial. My fault not theirs'. But they have all been great friends and, such is the dog-human relationship, more faithful than anyone deserves.

I look at the two old Labradors lying in front of the Aga. Fast asleep, their limbs twitch in memories of glorious days in the past. Ginny whimpers slightly. Perhaps she is remembering that day of high tides and gales when she ignored my whistle in order to prove that no duck which swam or dived had the beating of her. Peat stirs a grey muzzle as dreams of dogs, guns and men from Cornwall to Caithness fade in anticipation of a steady stroll down the lane, for all the world like a retired military man, taking his constitutional. 'Come on dogs, let's get the youngsters out of the kennel and see what the fields can produce.'

CHAPTER ONE

My Shooting Companions

MY PARENTS' HOME SITS ON TOP OF A HILL IN DUMFRIESSHIRE. IT OVER-looks the Nith estuary and, beyond, the Lakeland hills. Along the Scottish shore, Criffel provides a backdrop as it swells up into low clouds. As a teenager, I could lie in my bed on moonlit nights and hear goose music as the birds passed inland to feed.

A long and narrow farm stretches the mile from my parents' house to the River Nith; a fall of a few hundred foot. I was given a side-by-side, non-ejector 12-bore for my thirteenth birthday, following a succession of air rifles, and it was on that farm and with that gun that I learnt to shoot under my father's strict supervision. He had given up shooting during the war years, but had forgotten nothing about the ways of the quarry and the rules of safety. In fact, safety came first, middle and last. As a medical man, he had seen the devastation of ripped flesh and shattered bone intrinsic in a short range shooting accident, and he knew that a 'second chance' was not forthcoming in some cases.

When I became legally aged, at fifteen, to carry out my sorties un-accompanied, my father said that I had learned all he could show or tell me. I was on my own. Well, not quite on my own. My parents, in their wisdom, gave me a pup for my birthday. We called her Honey. The name reflected the nature as well as the colour of that attractive and kindly Labrador bitch bred in Glenfarg. A natural gundog, she steadfastly refused to be spoiled by my first hesitant attempts at training, with a whistle in one hand, and a book in the other. She was a delightful companion throughout my teenage years and into my twenties. I was devastated when my parents telephoned me at college to tell me that she had succumbed to a massive cancer. But when she was young she had been the first dog that I could truly call my own.

In those days with Honey on the farm, there were pheasants and partridges on the higher ground, with plenty of pigeons, rabbits and an occasional hare. Lower down, toward the river, I could bag duck and snipe on the Merse and from the ditches leading down to the still tidal river. On wild nights, when notherly gales tore at the trees, I would wait in ambush for flighting duck. In the very wildest weather, with exceptional luck, there was a change of a Greylag or Pinkfooted goose to enter in the game book, along with those that had been foolish enough to pass within range of my gun as they circled the still unploughed stubbles and potato fields upon their arrival on our shores.

January dusk with the rain beating horizontally in a never-ending sheet of spray out of inky-black clouds. A small skein came beating up in the half light. I realised my mistake in the second before I pulled the trigger. The family of Whooper swans flew on, so close that I might have felt the touch of their mighty wing beats.

Memories flood back. Creeping up to that bend in the ditch where the cattle drink. It was here that I shot a first right-and-left at snipe with the second and third cartridges that I fired from a 12-bore. And it was from that same spot that my first mallard sprang into a half-choke pattern of No. 6 shot. That was in the days before the arrival of Honey, so it was my job to squeeze and scratch my way through the thorn hedge in order to gather my prize. When I fetched the retrieve to my father, we took the time to sit and study the drake's handsome plumage. I plucked the black, metallic kiss-curl from its rump and tucked it into the band of my hat. I stroked the green sheen of its head and wondered at the marvel of it all. I felt not the slightest tinge of guilt as I tucked the drake's head beneath its wing and placed the still warm body in my game bag. Why feel guilty at being such a natural part of the country scene?

There is the tangle of driftwood at the river's edge where, one gale-torn evening in December, a small flight of tiny ducks came racing over my head. To my amazement, one of their number crumpled into a tumbling ball of feathers at my first shot. It fell with a splash into the river, and started to float away. It was followed a second later, by another, bigger splash and, a minute after that, Honey laid a teal drake in my hand.

THE PURSUIT OF SNIPE

One thing that none of the farm workers could ever understand was the pursuit of snipe. They would shake their heads in amazement to see us setting off across the Merse. With gun in hand, I would follow Honey's nose as she gently quartered close across my front. She was never so stupid as to think that she should try to catch the quarry herself. She knew that the kill was a job for me and the gun. She would tell me by her stance and quivering nose when game was afoot. On she would go, never more than 10yd (9m) in front of me, and always drinking in the air scent. Even then, with this well-behaved companion, I would often bless the long range combination of half and full choke when the snipe were skittish and, so long as I avoided zigging when the snipe was zagging, I would manage to knock down one or two.

What the farm workers could not understand was why I should waste an expensive cartridge on such a meagre morsel. Their intention was to shoot for the pot. On a farm worker's wage at that time, a hare or a mallard was a real prize, but not so the tiny snipe. In a similar vein, my father told me the tale of how he had learned to shoot straight. When staying with his cousin, on their hill farm close to Waterbeck in Dumfriesshire, the two boys would wage an unrelenting war on the vast rabbit

11

population. Uncle John's law was strict and simple. Two rabbits for every three cartridges that were issued, or else you had to pay for your own. And so the first rabbit would be shot sitting. The next one would be a sporting shot, taken as a rabbit bolted for cover. If that was killed, the next shot would also be at a running target but, if not, it would be back to taking a sitting pot-shot.

Given the many hundreds of rabbits they shot in a week, to be shipped off to the industrialised centres of middle England, it is not hard to understand why they were able to learn to shoot straight. And, in the long summer evenings, they would sharpen up their skills with a .22 rifle.

In these days of open-bored guns and small shot, it does no harm to think back to the ability and achievements of a generation raised on this style of shooting. I know men who think nothing of shooting bolting rabbits at 50yd (45m) range with a rifle, and each shot is through the head. An old highland gamekeeper of my acquaintance will, if invited, shoot walked-up grouse, one after another, with nothing more than the .22 that he has owned since he was a boy. But returning to snipe and why, despite their minimal proportions, they hold a place of esteem in my hunter's heart.

It may be that their appeal lies in their being such mysterious little birds. Also, the keen snipe shot is led to places where he might otherwise never venture. Perhaps I may be excused for likening them to the sea trout that draw so many to the lochs of the West Highlands and Hebrides, and the loughs of the West of Ireland. My little springer spaniel, a companion on most of my modern shooting escapades, was named Drummer as a mark of my affection for these 'will o' the wisps' of the shooting scene. Why 'Drummer'? What has this name got to do with snipe? Those who live in areas where snipe breed, and who have the eyes and ears of the countryman, will have heard the strange noise made by snipe that have flown to a not inconsiderable height in the skies. The noise they make as they descend is for all the world like a little drum.

Inspect a snipe and you will see that it has fourteen tail feathers. The two outside feathers are held rigidly out from the body as the bird descends, and it is the play of the air over these feathers that causes the noise. It might be presumed that this is part of their courtship display, except for the fact that both sexes drum, and that drumming can occur long before the mating season. So why do they do it? As I said earlier, snipe are mysterious little birds.

THE OLDER GENERATION

Incidentally, while craving indulgence for another digression, let me relate a little story that neatly dovetails the older generation of shooters with snipe. A few years ago, my father and I had snatched at an all too rare opportunity to get away together for a few days sea trout fishing in the Hebrides. We were sitting in the lounge of the hotel with two other guests; another father and son, who were a slightly older pair. The conversation came round to snipe and snipe shooting. The father complained that they had nothing like the numbers of snipe on their ground in Dorset as they had once had. The son, however, argued that there were just as many as there had ever been. At each turn of the conversation, the father grew more and more heated and was constantly cupping a hand to his ear and bellowing 'Eh? What? Speak up, for goodness sake boy,' while the 'boy', who was a very prosperous looking fifty year old, muttered about the silly old bugger refusing to wear a hearing aid.

'I blame it on the railways, you know!' said the old man.

'How on earth can it be their fault?' asked his son.

'Eh? What? Speak up!'

'Why the railways? shouted the son.

'Well, it's never been the same since they got rid of the old steam engines. There were always red-hot cinders flying out of

13

the old locomotives, and down they would come on the marsh when it was dry in the summer. That marsh used to be burnt regularly.'

'Yes, but why do you say there are less snipe nowadays?' asked the son.

'What? Eh?' roared the father.

'Why do you say there are less snipe?' screamed the son.

'Well, it's obvious, isn't it?' replied the old man. 'I never hear them drumming nowadays!'

Throughout my school years, and when I studied in Edinburgh, rough shooting and wildfowling remained my only involvement in the shooting world. Then I decided upon a shift in direction for my career. Having settled upon rural estate management, I knew that I would require a minimum of one year's practical experience before starting at the Royal Agricultural College. I was taken on at the Annandale Estates to spend four months with the forestry department, another four months on the farms, and then the rest of the year in the estate office. But, on the very first day, I was told to report to the head-keeper. This was my introduction to top quality, driven shooting. And I came to know it better, on two or three days a week throughout the pheasant season, with a stick rather than a gun in my hands.

Here was driven pheasant shooting in the best traditions of the sport. The majority of the guests were retired, high-ranking soldiers, some of whom had been brothers-in-arms with the present Earl's father. Some of them were accompanied by impeccably behaved gundogs, nearly all of which were black Labradors.

Gundogs were not encouraged in the beating line. The keepers would have their dogs, and keepers from neighbouring estates would attend to 'pick-up' those birds that fell well behind the line of guns, but beaters were expected to keep tapping their sticks, with their eyes and ears open for the keeper's instructions, and nothing else. But Honey would be waiting expectantly for me on my return. We would be out and about in no time, finding a bird or two to remind me that she was at least the equal of many of the dogs that I had seen during the day.

Some of the dogs whose work I witnessed all those years ago would put to shame some of the field trial champions that I have shot over in more recent times. And, believe me, in those days, few minded taking the time to watch and appreciate such dogs at work.

I met Carolyn, who was to become my wife, at the start of my second year at Cirencester. It was natural that I should propose to a girl who, when I asked what she would like best for a twenty-first birthday present, replied that she would like a black Labrador. And so, Ginny entered our lives. I have never known another dog that was so keen on water. Carolyn was living close to a loch at that time, and we always talked of taking Ginny for a swim, rather than a walk. For many years, if we were walking along a riverbank, Ginny would insist on swimming rather than walking with us. Only now that she is a teenager and, poor old girl, with two strokes behind her, does she prefer to stay dry.

We were visiting my sister, who was then living on an estate in Angus, when we met a young gamekeeper who simply had too many dogs in his kennels. The estate factor, who must have been a man without a soul, had told the keeper that some of the dogs must go. And that is how we came to return with a black-and-white springer spaniel bitch who answered to the name of Lady. She was a fine worker, but absolutely terrified at the sight of a gun. She was not gun shy as long as I stayed out of sight, I could fire a gun close to her and she would take no notice at all, except to cock her ears. The cure was found in propping a gun against the wall of the sitting room, night after night, while she was petted and stroked. In a few months, she was ready to take her place in the shooting field.

15

There is no need for dogs in some lines of beaters.

17

I left college, started work on the Buccleuch Estates at Langholm in Dumfriesshire, and married Carolyn, all within the space of a couple of months. Our wedding present to each other was Peat. As I look at him now, my memory races back to the day when we collected a little black butter-barrel of a dog puppy from the then Assistant Factor on the estate.

GROUSE AND WOODCOCK SHOOTING

Anyone who knows the history and statistics of grouse shooting in our islands will be aware that the moors of this estate produced the Scottish record bag, to a family party of the Duke's which included two young relations. There was, remarkably, a long delay at lunchtime, while a pony and trap was sent to collect fresh supplies of cartridges. Here was a perfect estate for a young, student factor keen on sport with rod, rifle and gun. It had a team of grouse keepers. The lowlands of the estate were divided into eight pheasant shoots, and each of these had a keeper. Three stalkers controlled the roe deer populations, and took out paying guests, mainly from continental Europe. A trio of River Watchers and a gillie saw to the association and private fishing on the Border Esk. Peat, however, never got a chance to join in the sport. Just at the time when he was maturing into a useful working dog, we packed up our belongings and moved to Cornwall.

On the new estate, where I was Assistant Land Steward, things were very different. For various reasons, it had been decided not to let any of the shooting. There was no game department. However, this did not mean that the estate staff and tenant farmers could not club together to make the most of what was on offer.

I talk of the estate but the holdings were, in fact, divided into a number of estates, manors and properties throughout the length and breadth of Cornwall. One estate in particular, close to Truro, became the centre of serious shooting effort because it had, under a previous ownership, been laid out and planted to provide sport with the quarry species for which Cornwall is justifiably famous. Talk of Cornwall to shooting folk, and they will immediately think of woodcock.

When I arrived on the estate, the Truro shoot had just gone through a period of transformation. The shooting had previously been mainly in the walked-up style, although with all the necessary subtleties and ruses required to bring about the woodcock's downfall. But now the accent was on driven sport. The tenant farmers were quite insistent that the 'young gentlemen' from the estate office should stand, rather than walk. So it was that Peat and I became what I felt were minor participants, while those tenants whose turn it was to walk the coverts, aided and abetted by keen local sportsmen with teams of excellent, close working springers and the occasional cocker spaniel, got on with the real sport. As you may gather from that statement, to me, woodcock shooting is a great deal more than a simple test of marksmanship. For those who revel in working dogs, know wild sport, and wish to be involved in the entire proceedings starting with the find and flush, the pulling of the trigger can become almost insignificant, except as a fitting end to the greater whole.

What level of sport did we enjoy with the Cornish woodcock? Well, they say that the Cornish are a secretive race, and there is certainly a code of silence where the 'cock shooting is involved. I was lucky enough to receive so much fine and open hospitality during my time there that I would never consider breaking that code. Suffice to say, perhaps, that if the Cornish do ever decide to become more open, there would have to be a quick rewriting of the record books.

But, as can so often happen, there was another side to the coin. We can all be guilty of imagining that the other man's grass is greener, and we may fail to appreciate what we have on our own doorstep. Certainly, on the great majority of shoots in Britain, where the pheasant necessarily provides the shooting man's staple sport, the woodcock is seen as a prize to be coveted. At the end of the day, when a hundred pheasants are laid out in the early fading light of a winter's evening, it will be the couple of woodcock that flushed from Jackson's Copse which will be the subject of discussion and congratulation.

But in Truro, things were different. Pheasants were thin on the ground, whereas woodcock might be plentiful. It was, therefore, the pheasants which were held up for admiration. Perhaps an analogy can be drawn with the attitude of the farm workers of my teenage experience, who could not understand why I should waste a cartridge on a snipe. Whatever, the end of our Cornish shoots always saw the farmers gathered into a huddle to discuss which honoured guest should receive the brace of pheasants, while the woodcock would be divided equally between the rest. It was perhaps inevitable, but nonetheless deeply regrettable in my opinion, that by the time we had spent our three years in Cornwall, and were ready to move on to new pastures, the tenants were talking about seven-week-old pheasant poults and release pens. A hundred pheasants were released in the year that I left. The following season, the number was far greater. The consequences were obvious. I heard from an old colleague that as surely as the pheasant numbers were increased, so the numbers of woodcock declined. The woodcock is a nocturnal bird which rests through the day. It can't get much rest if a load of noisy, interfering pheasants are strutting through the coverts and spinnies. That is why the old, true woodcock keepers would shoot a pheasant, sitting or flying, and record it in their list of 'vermin', if it had had the temerity to stray on to their ground. Still, the Cornish farmers seemed happy, and prepared to pay both capital and annual sums to replace what nature provided for free, with the gaudy and expensive import.

Packing our belongings and two Plymouth-born sons, we made the long trek to Argyll. On the way, we picked up Midge, a springer bitch puppy bred from impeccable field-trialing stock. She was a pretty and affectionate little soul, but to say that she was hyperactive would be an understatement. She would, perhaps, have excelled in the hands of a professional. She quartered the ground like a demon and would, without a doubt, have caught the judge's eye and then gone on to produce litter after litter of equally turbo-charged trialling dogs. But she was a nightmare to shoot over. She seemed to provide just two options. Either you worked her, giving her your full attention while a companion saw to the actual shooting, in much the same manner as a field trial, or else you tried to shoot over her yourself, accepting that she would be forever pushing to the limits so that you had either to give her constant attention, and let your shooting suffer, or be forever taking snapshots at fast departing, extreme range targets. Perhaps, in field trials, it would be no bad idea for the same person to have to shoot over as well as handle the dog. I do not know. But the problem of what to do with Midge was finally settled when she committed the ultimate sin for a Scottish country dog. She started showing an interest in sheep at lambing time.

Midge now lives with Carolyn's aunt and well away from sheep. She takes her walks, I should say gallops, along the beach at Ayr. But, whenever I see her setting off like a demented bumble-bee on heat, I look and wonder.

WATER SHYNESS

Argyll is hardly noted for its formal shooting, certainly not on its northern boundary with Inverness-shire, where we were living. Nevertheless, once you get to know the right places and people, you find that it can provide some excellent wild sport with grouse and woodcock in particular, as well as some outstanding duck

What finer sight than a brace of pointers working over the rolling, purple heather?

shooting.

It was because of the duck that I discovered a problem with Peat. He had matured into a lion-hearted, big black buck of a Labrador in the classic mould but, because all his work had been on inland shoots in Cornwall, he was not used to getting his feet wet. I had hardly taken any notice of his antics on Cornish beaches. In fact, I had almost kidded myself into believing that he paddled only into the water's edge when a stick was thrown because he recognised that Ginny, the watery wonder-dog, would invariably beat him to it. On her return to dry land, she would obligingly offer him one end of the stick, and they would carry it to me in perfect harmony, with neither one seeking to pull it from the other's grasp, for all the world like a shire horse and a thoroughbred in harness together!

My problem was that Peat was the experienced working dog, while Ginny remained Carolyn's pet and companion. The best solution seemed to be to try to capitalise on Peat's experience, rather than trying to teach Ginny a whole set of new tricks. But try as we might, we could not persuade Peat to get into the water. All those little dodges described in the best books on gundog training were proved useless in Peat's case. He simply stood his ground in three inches of water, and whined.

I discovered an ace up my sleeve. They say that Labradors are the greediest of dog breeds, and among Labradors, Peat was an outstanding glutton. The solution came to me in a flash. I called him to heel, picked up a packet of biscuits while Carolyn was not looking, and walked across the garden to the shore of the sea loch. Having tempted Peat with the biscuit, I threw it a few yards out onto the water. He did not hesitate. The next biscuit went 10yd (9m), and again he did not pause. The next one went 20yd (18m) and Peat threw up a mighty bow-wave in his rush to get at it.

The next biscuit was chucked with a truly mighty throw and it must have sunk by the time Peat had swum to its fall. He swam up and down, back and forth, and all over the loch in his search. I looked at my watch and sat down on a rock to wait for him. He kept swimming for ten minutes and, since that day, he has never looked back.

He must have learnt something from that biscuit which sank because today, if there is a crippled duck which insists on diving just before he gets to it, then he is quite happy to dive after it! Last season, a friend of mine was highly amused to see Peat ploughing along with his head under the surface of a shallow flight pond, in pursuit of a winged mallard drake. The old boy did look a bit funny to begin with, but not when his head reared up in a shower of spray, clutching the runaway.

My experiences in the Scottish Borders had all been with driven or walked-up grouse. However, in the Highlands, I was introduced to shooting grouse over pointers and setters. For those who combine the joys of dog work with those of shooting, there can surely be few finer sights than a brace of pointers working over the rolling oceans of purple heather. Skylarks soar over droning honey-bees in this perfect sporting scene, while a soft westerly breeze cools the brows of the tramping shooters. I have often wished that I could justify keeping and handling my own pointers or setters, but I can not. Nevertheless, it is one of the high points of my shooting year when I renew old acquaintances on the sparsely populated grouse moors where the formality and organisation of driven shooting is left aside.

Eventually, and now seven years ago, we returned to Dumfriesshire and I was able to return to shoot on the farm that runs from my parents' home down to the Nith. Indeed, I soon had the free run of a number of farms, and with my work and sport so closely intertwined, found myself in the glorious position of receiving invitations to visit a great number of shoots. Before long, too, I was elected a vice-president of the Solway Wildfowler's Association, whose interest in geese and duck extends down both the Scots and English shores of the Solway.

Peat was now in his element — up to a point. He had developed into my idea of an ideal companion for retrieving over land and water, but by no stretch of the imagination was he a hunting dog who could be relied upon to find and flush game. I wanted another spaniel, but with my experiences of Midge still fresh in my mind, I decided to bide my time.

A SHOOTING – MAN'S SPANIEL

I also became involved in a number of shoots as either a beater or picker-up, and I soon noted, as does everyone else in this neck of the woods, the outstanding work performed by one particular keeper with his team of spaniels. His dogs were clearly biddable, as well as hard-working, and he told me that this had as much to do with their breeding as with their training. So, when one of his bitches whelped in the following summer, I chose Drummer out of the litter. This merry little dog has taught me the true delights of shooting over a spaniel. He would never win a field trial. He doesn't set off hell-for-leather, because he knows the shooting day will see him running many miles over moor and through marsh, across ditch and dyke, burrowing through thorn and brambles here, and tussocks and bracken there. He is a stayer, not a sprinter, and that, surely, is what the shooting-man's spaniel should be — a dog that will not gallop, but one that trots and canters throughout the day.

But I very nearly lost him. By that I do not mean that he was nearly killed, however, but he was very nearly spoilt as a spaniel for shooting over due, very largely, to my own thoughtlessness. In his first season of work, I decided that he would gain quickly in experience by being taken beating on various pheasant shoots in this area. It would also make him steady to the flush of game, as it would not be getting shot over him. That was the theory.

To begin with, his summer training was clearly proving itself. He worked his ground in copy book style, quartering across never more than 10yd (9m) to my front or 20yd (18m) to either side. If he scented a pheasant lurking in a pile of brashing or clump of brambles, he would be in at it like a terrier at a rat, except that he kept his jaws closed. When we got close to the end of a covert, where pheasants had concentrated, he would not rush forward and throw them up in one almighty flush to the consternation of the waiting guns. And I liked to think that the keepers on the shoots were starting to notice him because we were steadily being given more responsible tasks to perform. A description of one of these tasks will, perhaps, serve to show where and when the rot started to set in.

At one drive on a certain estate, pheasants were flushed over a deep valley between two coverts. The the second covert was driven out. Obviously, the birds from the first drive could not immediately be picked, as it would ruin the second drive. And so I was put with Drummer to walk down the side of the wood, with a keeper and his two spaniels on my right. When we emerged at the end of the wood, we had to call out for help from the other beaters to carry the slain. We had picked over forty pheasants between us. Drummer had picked fifteen on his own, and it was a relatively short wood.

At the next drive, the little dog, who previously would have moved heaven and earth to flush a bird, ran past squatting birds. I realised he had got it into his tiny mind that his job was now to fetch the slain, rather than flush the living. Equally, because on some of the larger shoots there were so many birds on the ground, his hunting was becoming 'slapdash' as if he were thinking 'Oh well, if I miss one, there will be another in a few yards.'

Then he started picking up bad habits from those dogs that seem to know when the boss' eye is off them, and make the most of the opportunity to run riot. On another occasion, an aggressive Labrador pounced on the little chap and snatched away the bird that he was retrieving. Do I need to say any more?

Drummer no longer joins in the beating line, and if he does appear on a formal shoot, it will only be when I am either shooting or picking-up. Drummer 'hoovers' up the birds that have fallen close to the guns' positions, while Peat busies himself with the longer range retrieves. But a dog's life is all too short and Peat, although I would never say so to his face, is starting to feel his age. Afternoon drives now find him trotting out and walking back on his retrieves. And while I will still happily take him out to the duck ponds for the evening flight, knowing that he will soon be home to the warm and dry of the fireside while I clean the gun and take a dram, I could never be so cruel as to take him out for long hours below the sea wall when the Scottish winter is showing its worst. So now we have Drake, who has been with us for nearly a year. He is still little more than a puppy, a great lolloping clown with a smile on his big, black face. Still, he has the makings of the right stuff even if time alone will tell.

That has brought me to the present day. Looking back, it strikes me just how many of my shooting companions have been left out. I have been lucky to know a whole assortment of dogs and shooting men throughout the length and breadth of our islands: in Scotland, Ireland, England and Wales. Some have been paragons of virtue, others have been total rascals, but nearly all of them, like a son is to his mother, have been the apple of someone's eye. This is only an introductory chapter, and closer meetings will have to wait for later pages. But, before we can look further at the role of the sporting dog in the shooting scene, we must look more closely at the history of the sport, in order to see how the duties of gundogs have evolved.

Charles St. John added blackcock to his game bag.

CHAPTER TWO

Two Centuries of Gundogs

IN ORDER FULLY TO UNDERSTAND THE ROLE OF THE VARIOUS BREEDS of gundogs to be seen in the modern shooting scene, it helps enormously to understand the development of shooting as a sport over the last two centuries. We are then able to see why some breeds have risen in popularity, while others have fallen into eclipse. Driven shooting, or *battue* shooting as it was originally called, was introduced to Britain little more than one hundred years ago. How was shooting conducted before that time?

In the early years of the nineteenth century, sportsmen were armed with muzzle-loaders, either flintlock or percussion cap, and leaving the pursuit of duck and geese aside for the time being, had the option of walking either with or without dogs. One writer, who left a vivid account of what might be achieved in those days by a sportsman with time, wealth and a love of adventure in wild places, was Charles St. John.

The parish register of Chailey in Sussex records the birth of a son on 3 December 1809. Charles William George St. John was in fact the fifth son of General the Hon. Frederick St. John, a grandson of the first Viscount Bolingbroke. Charles' mother was a daughter of Lord Craven, the Hon. Arabella Craven before her marriage. You might say that Charles was born with something of a silver spoon in his mouth but, as a fifth son, he had to make his own way in life.

After attending school at Midhurst in Sussex, he entered the

Treasury as a clerk at the age of nineteen. His future was assured. However, despite the fact that he was able to spend some of his spare time shooting duck and snipe over boggy ground in Knightsbridge, now the site of Harrods', and pursuing blackgame on the still undeveloped Surrey heathlands, by the age of twenty-one, he had had enough. He could not stand the prospect of London for one day longer.

Luckily for the young St. John, his cousin, the third Viscount Bolingbroke, had a property at Rosehall in Sutherland, which provided the ideal base for a man seeking a maximum of sport and a minimum of work. If St. John harboured any worries as to his future income, these were removed when, at the age of twenty-five, he married the daughter of a banker from Newcastle-upon-Tyne, whose wealth was combined with a love of the country life and a preparedness to live in what was still an extremely remote area of the realm.

For the next twenty years, St. John was free to indulge both his love of wild sports with rod, rifle and gun, and his thirst for knowledge of natural history. Both facets of his character shine out from the pages of his book *The Wild Sports and Natural History of the Highlands*.

Just one passage will serve to illustrate the style of sport enjoyed by St. John, and to quicken the heart of any true sportsman who anticipates or knows the joy of shooting over his own dogs:

> *October 20th   Determined to shoot across to Malcolm's shealing, at the head of the river, twelve miles distant; to sleep there; and kill some ptarmigan the next day.*
>
> *For the first mile of our walk we passed through the old fir woods, where the sun seldom penetrates . . . As we were just leaving the wood a woodcock rose, which I killed. Our way took us up the rushy course of a burn. Both dogs came to a dead point near the stream, and then drew for at least quarter of a mile, and just as my patience began to be*

exhausted, a brace of magnificent old blackcocks rose, but out of shot. One of them came back right over our heads at a good height, making for the wood. As he flew quick down the wind, I aimed nearly a yard ahead of him as he came towards me, and down he fell, fifty yards behind me, with a force that seemed enough to break every bone in his body. Another and another blackcock fell to my gun before we had left the burn, and also a hare, who got up in the broken ground near the water. Our next cast took us up a slope of hill, where we found a wild covey of grouse. Right and left at them the moment they rose, and killed a brace; the rest went over the hill. Another covey on the same ground gave me three shots. From the top of the hill we saw a dreary expanse of flat ground, with Loch A-na-caillach in the centre of it, a bleak cold-looking piece of water, with several small grey pools near it. Donald told me a long story of the origin of its name, pointing out a large cairn of stones at one end of it. The story was, that some few years ago, . . .

But where are the dogs all this time? There they are, both standing, and evidently at different packs of grouse. I killed three of these birds, taking a right and left shot at one dog's point, and then going to the other.

Off went Old Shot now, according to his usual habit, straight to a rushy pool. I had him from a friend in Ireland, and being used to snipe shooting, he preferred it to everything else. The cunning old fellow chose not to hear my call, but made for his favourite spot. He immediately stood, and now for the first time seemed to think of his master, as he looked back over his shoulder at me, as much as to say, 'Make haste down to me, here is some game'. And sure enough up got a snipe, which I killed. The report of my gun putting up a pair of mallards, one of which I winged a long way off, 'Hie away, Shot' and Shot, who was licensed to take such liberties, splashed in with great

*glee, and after being lost to sight for some minutes among
the high rushes, came back with the mallard in his mouth.
'A bad lesson for Carlo that, Master Shot,' but he knows
better than to follow your example. We now went up the
opposite slope leaving Loch A-na-caillach behind us, and
killing some grouse and a mountain hare, with no white
about her as yet. We next came to a long stony ridge, with
small patches of high heather. A pair of ravens rising from
the rocks, soared croaking over us for some time. A pair or
two of old grouse were all we killed here. But the view from
the summit was splendidly wild as we looked over a long
range . . .*

And so Charles St. John and Donald continued on their
way, the two pointers working ahead of them. Donald,
incidentally, was St. John's gillie in the truest sense; a paid man,
yes, but a sporting companion rather than any sort of a servant.
Finally, they are closing on their destination.

*We killed several more grouse and a brace of teal.
Towards the afternoon we struck off to the shepherd's
house. In the fringe of a birch that sheltered it, we killed a
blackcock and a hen, and at last got to the end of our walk
with fifteen brace of grouse, five black game, one mallard,
a snipe, a woodcock, two teal and two hares; and right
glad was I to ease my shoulder of that portion of the game
which I carried to help Donald, who would at any time
have preferred assisting me to stalk a red deer than to kill
and carry grouse. Although my day's sport did not amount
to any great number, the variety of game, and the beautiful
and wild scenery I had passed through, made me enjoy it
more than if I had been shooting in the best and easiest
muir in Scotland, and killing fifty or sixty birds.*

Charles St. John was one of the first sporting writers to set
out so clearly the attractions of the mixed bags for which
Scotland had, and has, virtually no rivals. In later years, the

Purdey brothers were to speak of mixed Scottish bags in their book *The Shotgun* and many still regard Scotland in October as the place and time to discover a shooting paradise.

Later in this book St. John goes on to describe another October day when a tremendous variety ended up being noted down in his game-book. Together with his pointer, he had a retriever out for

> *a few hours' walk, and on a most stormy windy day. I had promised to send a hamper of game to a friend in Edinburgh, and knowing that he would prize it more if I could make up a variety than if I sent him double the quantity of any one kind, I determined to hunt a wild part of my shooting-ground, where I should have a chance of finding ducks, snipes . . .*

And how he succeeded is shown in the following extract from his game-book:

Grouse	6	Teal	1
Partridge	13	Curlew	3
Woodcock	1	Plover	4
Pheasant	1	Jacksnipe	2
Wild duck	1	Hare	5
Snipe	4	Rabbit	2

UNPROFESSIONAL BEHAVIOUR

It is interesting to note St. John's description of his pointer, Shot, ignoring commands and setting off on his own to inspect a rushy pool. The majority of professional trainers would heavily censure such behaviour. However, St. John, as a shooting man, was obviously prepared to forgive this act of mutiny, no doubt influenced by the fact that it led to an extra snipe and a mallard in the bag. He alerts his readers to the fact that some of the normally specialist pointer breeds are, as individuals, quite capable of making their own retrieves. And, as if it explained everything, he had the dog from a friend in Ireland. Old dogs, just like humans, have their tastes, traits and foibles. One of my own dogs, if ordered to hunt a hedge for pheasants on my left, when faced with a tussocky, marshy area on my right which might harbour a snipe, will show his preference to the point where I am eventually forced to replace the No.6 shot with No.8. Utterly disgraceful, the professional would say, but I suppose it all depends upon whether dogs are viewed as shooting companions or robotic servants.

Having mentioned St. John's pointer from Ireland, it is fair to explain that its remote and untamed west coast offered an even greater challenge to the sportsman-adventurer than the Scottish Highlands at that time. It was a long road from Dublin to Ballycroy, and not a welcoming one according to one writer:

> The grave offences with which these wild people are principally charged appear to be abduction and murder; and both are of frequent recurrence. The first, indeed, is so prevalent, that any lady bent upon celibacy had better avoid Ballycroy, and particularly so if she has obtained the reputation of being opulent.

That description is taken from a classic of Irish sporting literature, *Wild Sports of the West of Ireland* by William Hamilton Maxwell, which first appeared in 1832 and painted a picture of the sport of the time. It also included much of the 'legendary tales, folk-lore, local customs and natural history', of a land and people who, to the English reader of the time, might have seemed as remote as the Hindu-Kush or Karamajong. Young ladies of high virtue and wealth would have quaked at the prospect of being secreted in the mountains, beyond the reach of the authorities or concerned friends, to be 'left at the mercy of the ruffian and his confederates, until they are at last obliged to become the legal property of the despoiler'.

Maxwell's wooing was certainly not so rough in style as that of the wild men of the west but, once he had 'made a good match', there is no doubt that he led his wife, as they say, 'one hell of a life'. His books might paint a picture of some sort of boy's own comic-strip hero, but the truth behind the story is one of a man who was, in the words of an earlier generation, a 'cad, bounder, poseur and waster', who ended his days as a penniless alcoholic in Musselburgh, Scotland, long after his wife and family had given him up as a lost cause.

But enough of the plights of rich maidens and poor, suffering wives. Whatever might be said about him, Maxwell was a fine writer and left a notable account of the sport he enjoyed with his companions and retainers. In many ways, his sport reflected that of St. John. Certainly, they both relied heavily upon the pointer and setter breeds to show them sport to their muzzle-loaders.

Of course, the English sportsman did not have to travel to Scotland or Ireland to enjoy sport with native game species. The possibilities in England at that time were described by Lieutenant Colonel Peter Hawker. *Instructions to Young Sportsmen* was established as 'the shooting man's Bible' in the early decades of the nineteenth century.

Hawker may be best remembered for his advice on duck, guns and punts, but he also had a great deal to say about the game shooting of the time. Indeed, of the total of 17,753 head that he shot between 1802 and 1853, 7,035 were partridges. He also bagged 2,116 snipe. His writing reveals that, like St. John and Maxwell, he relied heavily on pointers to provide this sport. He also mentions spaniels, however, for use on the more enclosed lands of the southern country. Many a modern-day spaniel enthusiast will smile at these words of Hawker's:

> With regard to spaniels, they are, nine times in ten, so badly broken in, as, in general, to be only fit to drive a large wood; but, if taught to keep always within half a gunshot they are the best dogs in existence for working among hassocks and briars.

So what has changed?

Hawker also introduced his readers to a newly imported breed of dog, arriving from the Canadian maritime provinces of Newfoundland and Labrador. He described them as being of two types and said that:

> . . . by far the best for every kind of shooting, is oftener black than of another colour, and scarcely bigger than a pointer. He is made rather long in the head and nose; pretty deep in the chest; very fine in the legs; has short or smooth hair; does not carry his tail so much curled as the other; and is extremely quick and active in running, swimming and fighting . . . may be broken in to any kind of shooting; and, without additional instruction, is generally under such command, that he may safely be kept in, if required to be taken out with pointers. For finding wounded game, of every description, there is not his equal in the canine race; and he is a sine qua non in the general pursuit of wildfowl.

So there we have an early description of the appearance, character and role of the breed that was to emerge as the most popular breed of gundog. In fact, virtually nothing more needs to be said in describing the Labrador of today. Some modernists may take exception to the words 'quick and active in fighting' but not, believe me, if they have ever witnessed or tried to separate a pair of fighting Labradors on a shoot day, and seen the damage they can inflict upon each other in the shortest space of time. This is particularly so among those Labradors which spend most of their time in canine rather than human company; dogs that are pushed away into a kennel and forgotten about except on shoot days.

The Labrador's role was seen at that time, except on wildfowling expeditions, as being an easily trained dog to 'be kept safely in' at heel, while the sportsman walked, often behind his pointers. Remember, too, that Charles St. John was accompanied by a steady retriever, although he does not say of what breeding, as well as his pointers on that 'few hours' walk, and on a most stormy and windy day', when he had promised to send a hamper of mixed game to a friend in Edinburgh. But there is absolutely no mention from St. John, Maxwell or Hawker of the retriever's role as so many modern-day shooting-men would see it; retrieving the slain and wounded at the end of a drive. The reason is obvious. Driven shooting had not been introduced to our islands, in any notable form, at the time when these three sportsmen were writing.

THE 'GREAT SHOOTS'

It was a combination of factors that led to what some choose to describe as the 'Great Shoots' of the late Victorian, Edwardian and Georgian eras. For one thing, the beginnings of intensive game production was added to the older and rather crude methods of game preservation. And farming practices had not yet developed to the stage at which wild populations of game birds would be discouraged. The railways opened up the remoter parts of our lands, so that a sportsman might travel to previously far away places, shoot for three or four days, and return to London, all in the space of one week.

Equally, the sporting gun had developed from its original, muzzle-loading form into the double-barrelled, breech-loading and hammerless ejector, identical to those that we use today. Such guns might be ordered and made as a pair, so that the sportsman's rate of fire could be increased with the aid of a loader. In extreme cases, a 'garniture' of three virtually identical guns could be used with the services of two loaders and a cartridge boy. Such a combination might shoot with the same slick and deadly efficiency as a naval gunnery team.

The whole shooting scene, for those who were prepared and able to indulge in the new, driven style, was transformed. It is not insignificant that this occurred at a time when fortunes were being made in 'trade', and massively elaborate shooting parties were one way in which old and new-found wealth could be flaunted in a socially acceptable fashion, with Royal participation, as well as its nod of approval. The upshot was that neighbour might vie with neighbour to provide even bigger and, they thought, better bags.

By the closing years of the century, a number of shoots were seeking to build their names upon the fact that they could provide a stream of birds sufficient for a crack-shot of the day to have four pheasants dead in the air at the same time, or ten grouse in ten seconds, tumbling into the heather around a single butt.

But despite the obsession of some sporting historians with this type of shoot and style of shooting, it was still very much a minority affair, and many of the sportsmen of the time were strongly against it. The letter pages of sporting and country magazines at the turn of the century were filled with debate, argument and even heated, personal exchanges as to whether driven or *battue* shooting could even be described as a sport. Take, for example, the following passage, lifted from a late-nineteenth century editorial article that appeared in the *Field* magazine:

> It is for the purpose of the battue *that pheasants are now reserved and preserved with all the formidable retinue of head-keepers* . . . No one can deny the fitness of the pheasant for affording gratification to the good sportsman if the bird is fairly found, put up and shot; but as well might mobbing a fox be called fox-hunting as a battue *be considered genuine pheasant shooting.*

Then, as so often happens today, the writer decided to be a little more personal, and introduced a note of hysteria:

> In the battue *nothing short of hundreds, or, if possible, thousands of killed, to say nothing of wounded, will*

constitute a successful day. The pseudo-sportsman, who should he be tempted from his Times and his fireside for anything under five brace an hour, would be inclined to complain, and would think, if he did not say, that his presence had been obtained under false pretences. The mode usually adopted is as follows: –

First get together eight or ten crack shots, who may, many of them, be in wheeled chairs, or on shooting ponies . . . Domestic poultry must be reared and killed, but who would admit the pleasure of wringing their necks or cutting their throats? Yet where lies the difference? The pheasant is not even a difficult shot.

Is it necessary to state that these words were obviously penned by somebody who was not all knowledgeable on the subject? Certainly, teams of the best performers with a gun might be brought together, but this keen and dedicated circle of sportsmen hardly needed to be transported in wheeled chairs or on the back of ponies. Many of them were absolute sticklers in matters of health and fitness. They could not maintain their reputations if they stayed up to eat, drink, smoke and flirt on the night before a big shoot, and they could not afford to be feeling the pace after firing perhaps four or five hundred cartridges before lunch. Right or wrong, these men shot to a standard that is rarely seen today. And, as to whether or not the pheasant was a difficult shot, nobody was better qualified than these to offer an expert opinion.

In April, 1905, the *Badminton Magazine* printed replies received to the question 'Which is the most difficult shot?' which had been put to a team of the best-known shooting men of that era. All but one or two of them stated that it was the driven pheasant, with the proviso in nearly all cases that it should be truly high, and perhaps curling, dropping and planing on set wings. Now, I have heard folk say that those Edwardians did not know what they were talking about, because driven pheasants

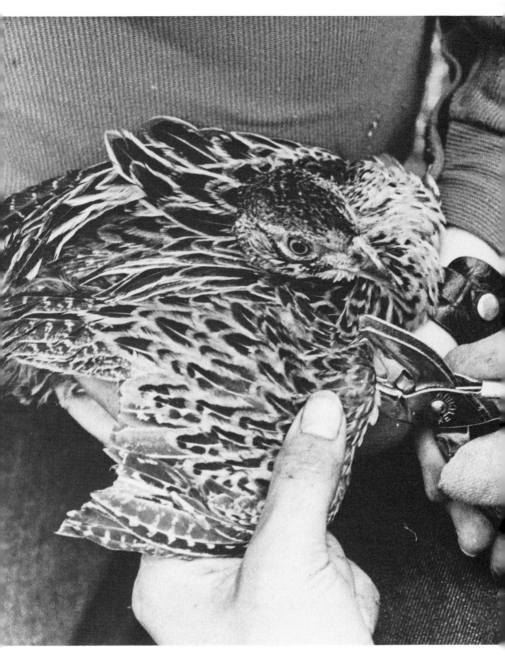

It seems inevitable that reared and released pheasants should be likened to domestic poultry.

were all they ever shot. Well, just to knock that rumour on the head, consider the case of Earl de Grey, later to become the Marquess of Ripon. His reply was that he believed the most difficult shot to be: 'A high pheasant coming down wind with a drop and a curl'. He had shot more than 100,000 of them, but what did he have to compare them with? His other totals encompassed 47,468 grouse, 89,401 partridges, more than a couple of thousand each of woodcock and snipe, 26,417 hares, 26,747 rabbits, thousands of duck, not to mention the two rhinoceros, eleven tigers and 8,424 various.

Incidentally, I quote these figures only to illustrate that men such as Lord de Grey knew what they were talking about, although words would fail to describe my own feelings at such a tally of death.

I remember fishing a West Highland loch in the company of a gillie who had not spoken a word other than Gaelic until he went to the school. He was also a stalker. As we drifted the shore, trying to tempt a salmon or sea trout to rise to a team of Dunkeld, Mallard and Claret and Black Pennel flies, he fixed me with his clear blue eyes and told me of the nightmares that he had been suffering. A few months previously, he had counted the number of stags entered in his personal stalking diary, and realised that he was only a couple short of the thousand. Ever since, he had been troubled with this same dream, night after night. He was alone on the high hills and came to the edge of a corrie. He looked down into its depths, where a thousand stags lay . . .

Perhaps the story needs to be told by a Highlander to another with Highland blood from his paternal grandmother but I have not entered any numbers in my game-books since that time. I can tell you who I was with on such and such a day, what the weather was like, how the dogs performed or what flies were successful; I can even tell you what we had for lunch and tea; but do not ask how many we shot or caught because the answer is that I simply do not know!

DRIVEN SHOOTING

But I have digressed from a consideration of how the introduction of driven shooting altered the role, or created new roles, for gundogs in the shooting scene. There was a long argument on the pros and cons of driven shooting and interesting snippets that point toward changing attitudes can be drawn from the correspondence.

Lord Walsingham was drawn into the debate after he had shot the phenomenal bag of 1,070 grouse in one day, to his own gun, on his moor at Blubberhouse in Yorkshire. Although 'to his own gun' he was, of course, accompanied by two loaders to handle the four guns that he employed, all Purdey breechloaders, all having 30in, cylinder barrels and firing 1oz. of No.5 Derby shot. And there were plenty of beaters to drive the grouse over Walsingham's butt.

The ensuing debate brought to light a number of interesting factors. One was a clear indication of the increased bags that could be shot on a moor when driving was introduced. Between the years 1829 and 1843, the Blubberhouse Gamebook reveals that minimums of twelve and fourteen and a half brace, and maximums of ninety brace in 1835 and ninety-one brace in 1843 were shot in one season.

After that, the records were incomplete until 1865, a few seasons after a little 'mild' driving had been introduced, when 289 brace were accounted for. The following season produced 691 brace, 1870 produced 478, and 1872 ended with 807½ brace, and so on and so forth, with the peaks and troughs inherent to any grouse moor, leading up to the season that has gone down in history when Lord Walsingham shot his record bag and during which a total of 1,786 grouse (893 brace) were shot on a total area of only 2,221 acres.

How did Lord Walsingham see dogs in his scheme of things? The following remarks are from a long letter that he wrote to *Land and Water* magazine, which was published on 19 October, 1888 under the heading, 'Is Driving Sport?':

> *I have no hesitation in saying that on any English moor of, say 2,000 to 4,000 acres, persistent moderate driving or persistent dogging or walking would yield poorer results in numbers in the long run than two or three big days at the best moment, supplemented by a judicious picking-off of outside birds whenever the weather is favourable. Thus any other plan would be in greater or less degree wasteful, and therefore less sportsmanlike.*

It should be noted that Walsingham, in his definition of sportsmanship, alluded to securing 'the maximum of enjoyment consistent with bringing to book the largest number of birds the ground can be made to yield without unduly diminishing the breeding stock'. I cannot help commenting that we might nowadays see this not so much as sportsmanship but as good shoot management and sensible husbandry in order to produce the maximum yield. Whatever, let us see what else Lord Walsingham had to say relating specifically to gundogs:

> *I have walked after grouse on Blubberhouse Moors till my nose bled, and all the keepers took off their coats, and that in the days of dogs, simply because I got more shots by doing so than if I waited for about two points in every three hours, while birds were constantly topping the skyline . . .*
>
> *I also fully admit that to see good pointers or setters carefully quartering the ground enhances the pleasure of shooting even to a greater degree than mere exercise of the lungs and sinews; but if one feels that the system involves waste of time and opportunities, and disturbs a vastly larger number of birds than it enables him to approach, he should at least not despise other methods requiring greater skill and more cunning, while insuring larger results.*

That must be one of the neatest, back-handed compliments ever seen in print. Walsingham continues:

I am confident that on all Yorkshire moors, a really good walker can kill more grouse without pointers or setters than with them, so long as he behaves fairly by his dogs and gives them time to work their ground. If he uses dogs, he must keep within sight of them, and, as his head is always higher than the dog's, the birds can see him a greater distance, and as soon as Yorkshire grouse see a man after August 25 – and in most seasons much earlier – they move off . . .

. . . but, again, I say a good walker, if he knows his ground and shoots equally well, will beat any man with dogs. He loses the pleasure of seeing the dogs work, but has himself to exercise sagacity instead of leaving the dogs to do it for him . . .

Other than admitting, almost grudgingly, that pointers and setters were pretty to watch, did Walsingham have nothing to say in their favour?

There are many places where game is scarce in which dogs are unquestionably of the greatest use. A forty-acre field, with but one or two coveys of partridges in it, taxes the patience of those who undertake to find them without such help. The large, open fields of rough grass on the borders of the fen lands in Norfolk and Cambridgeshire, unless richly stocked with birds, would show the use of a brace of good pointers. The ground can be covered in less than half the time it would take to get over without them. On many Scotch moors, thinly stocked, where grouse lie far better early in the season than they do in England, setters or pointers are of great advantage, especially to a solitary sportsman. But why should anyone be thought not to understand the real business of sport because he declines to adopt a method by which hundreds can be bagged in places where thousands can be got by other means, and that not once in a way, but year after year on the same ground?

Lord Walsingham, if dismissive of the use of pointers or setters on moors such as Blubberhouse, was however keen to point out that they still involved pleasures for the man keen to work his dogs:

Good retrievers are wanted, and I know no better training for a young dog than to let him work with a couple of good, steady, but experienced older ones. It teaches him to be quick in the return, bringing bird after bird, as long as they are easily found and seeking diligently in a spirit of rivalry when there are but few left to gather. There is usually plenty for all to do, and by the end of a drive a running bird will often have reached a distance of two hundred yards or more, giving a dog every chance of showing his quality.

Perhaps that is enough from Lord Walsingham. Another shooting man of the time, who figured in the record books, was Sir Frederick Millbank. He was one of a party of six, shooting Wemmergill Moor on 20 August, 1872. The total bag of grouse for the day was 1,035 brace, of which Sir Frederick personally shot 364 brace with his three guns and two loaders, in the eight drives. It goes without saying that a man who was regularly involved in shoots that might produce this scale of shooting, would have a clear idea as to the best dog for the job. The following extract is from a letter that he wrote to *Shooting* magazine, published on 26 September, 1888.

Just a few words . . . as to picking up birds. In thick heather it is a difficult job, especially on a hot, still day. I read last year of a plan of marking the places where the birds fall. This may be done when you kill a few brace at a stand, but it is totally impossible when you fire as quickly as you can take the guns from the loaders. How about eight birds to the minute? No, the only plan is to trust to your man and dogs. I have always used spaniels that retrieve well – I find they are twice as quick as the large retriever; their noses

45

Sir Frederick Millbank chose spaniels for their speed in picking up grouse.

being near the heather, they pick up birds in an incredibly short time, and never tire if well bred. I have observed the best large retrievers, and the more I see of them the more covinced I am that the spaniel is the right dog for the purpose; generally I have two of them in my stand, and I rarely ever lose a bird . . .

. . . the more thoroughly broken the big retriever is, the worse he is for finding grouse. I am now speaking as to the time; it is a great advantage to have your birds picked up as quickly as possible, and then off for another drive. My practice is to have five or six of these spaniels out, two with me and the rest with a man to help my friends.

Here, Sir Frederick Millbank has described another role being introduced for the spaniel. Today, it is common to see teams of spaniels 'hoovering-up' birds that have fallen close to the butts, or pegs on a pheasant or partridge shoot. They really can excel at this work although, on a longer range retrieve, perhaps on a pricked bird, my own money would be on the 'big retriever'. And the question of whether or not this style of retrieving is conducive to spaniels whose duties may, the following day, require them to hunt never more than 20yd from the gun is also open to debate. So, perhaps, this is as good a place as any to close this broad consideration of the gundogs' changing role in the shooting scene, and take a closer look at various shooting situations, the problems they present, and the dogs which can provide the solutions.

Spaniel puppies — born and bred to hunt, flush and retrieve relatively sparse populations of game.

Another place, another young gun who, like the author, learns the joy of shooting over dogs.

Pickers-up on a formal shooting day.

Tiring but unforgettable sport in the West Highlands.

Charles St. John's retriever may well have been a flatcoat like this one.

Pointer in 'classic' pose — but Lord Walsingham argued against their use on his moors.

'Ladies and dogs are welcome, if kept under strict control.'

A picker-up with his spaniel standing well behind the line of guns.

Spaniels at a driven shoot.

Generally speaking a retriever excels on long-distance retrieves, while a spaniel 'hoovers' up the closer birds.

CHAPTER THREE

Dogs on the Formal Shoot

THOSE WHOSE EXPERIENCE, HOWEVER EXTENSIVE, IS LIMITED TO standing at a peg on the formal, driven pheasant shoot, or in a butt on the grouse moor, may have little if any idea of the true value of a good dog. Their knowledge may extend no further than the situations described in the words of Lord Walsingham and Sir Frederick Millbank in the previous chapter, in which those birds that have been shot during the course of a drive have to be gathered with maximum efficiency, and in minimum time. In fact, truth be told, there are many members of many shooting parties of the driven kind whose knowledge of dogs and even the quarry species, extends no further than they would need to join in a corporate day's entertainment on a clay-pigeon ground.

This might be said to be symptomatic of what sociologists describe as the 'redistribution of wealth' throughout the twentieth century. It started with a hardcore of the very wealthiest of men who could afford to shoot three or four or more days a week throughout the season and whose interests, as the game records of men such as Lord de Grey show, extended from pheasant, grouse and partridge to snipe, woodcock and duck. Quite simply, these men had the time and money to become completely immersed in their sport. In recent times, I would suggest, the great majority of driven game shooters have had but ten days of sport, between November and January, and it has been rare to be able to add the spice of variety to a staple diet of reared and released pheasants. However, as we enter the closing decade of the century, although the pheasant remains the backbone of British sport, there are clear signs of a renewed interest in the alternative forms of shooting, with travelling syndicates perhaps dropping a couple of pheasant days in order to allow them to travel north for a few days either walking on the moors, or rough shooting and wildfowling. Leaving other considerations aside, what effect has this had on gundogs?

Success in rough shooting depends very heavily upon the quality of the dogs involved be they spaniels, pointers and setters, or one of the continental hunter-pointer-retriever breeds. In wildfowling, while the dog may not be involved in providing the shot for its master it can, in most cases, be seen as essential in gathering the slain.

But formal, driven shooting relies first and foremost on management and organisational ability. Dogs take on a minor role and it is not outside the bounds of imagination to picture a driven pheasant shoot conducted without any form of canine assistance. This has led to the situation where shooting people who happen to be keen to use a dog, and own a good retriever, feel that they must ask their host's permission to bring it along. Equally, I have seen a shooting invitation that expressly stated: 'Ladies and dogs are welcome, if kept under strict control, but please give notice so that we can make the necessary arrangements for lunch.'

However, the keen dog-owner who is upset at having to leave their canine companion at home, or who senses a prevailing mood that suggests he must ignore the 'runner' that planed down, carrying a leg, must realise that there is more than one side to the coin. It may not simply be that his fellow guns take no interest in dogs and prefer to give their whole attention to the actual shooting. It could, alternatively, be that his host is suffering from 'once bitten, twice shy-itis' having had to suffer a fool and his dog in the past.

Anyone with some experience of driven shooting will be able

to quote examples of the upsets and problems caused by apparently untrained and uncontrollable dogs. In an extreme case, a dog may have run into the best drive of the day, flushing birds hither and tither as it chased about, blind and deaf to its oh-so-embarrassed owner. This extends through to more minor irritations, such as the dog which is loosed at the end of a drive and tears about picking a pheasant here, dropping it in favour of another one there, to the point where everyone is thoroughly confused and no-one has a clue as to what birds remain to be picked. This sort of behaviour can have its darker side. There are jealous, greedy shots with jealous, greedy dogs that gather throughout a drive so that, at its end, the owner can stand with an idiot grin in front of a heap of birds as if he had shot them all. A strange sort of behaviour – ensure that he is left to carry them all as well.

Rather than dwelling on bad dogs, and their indifferent or irritating behaviour, a more positive approach would be to look at the organisation of a driven shoot with a view to establishing those areas where good dogs can prove their worth, as well as enhancing the overall enjoyment of the day. Because, despite my 'devil's advocacy' in the opening passages of this chapter, when I suggested the possibility of a 'no-dog-shoot', the truth is that most shoots depend very heavily upon the services of good dogs.

Reduced to its absolute basics, the organisation of a driven shooting day can be seen as three distinct operations. The basics do not alter whatever the quarry. Firstly, a team of unarmed beaters flush the game in such a manner that they fly over the team of waiting guns. Secondly, this team of guns endeavour to shoot said game. Finally, the game which has been shot is gathered. It is from these basics that we can identify and evaluate the role that dogs might play.

BEATERS' DOGS

At the turn of the century, during the days of the 'Great Shoots', the countryside was still heavily populated compared with today's situation. When my grandfather gave up one of the family farms at the start of the depression after the First World War, there were 120 souls; men, women and children; living upon it. Today, there are eight. This may serve to create some impressions of the very great numbers of staff and their families who lived on much larger estates, rather than farms, at that time; staff who, quite probably, would not be fully 'utilised' on farm, forestry and maintenance work during the autumn and winter months of the shooting season. Thus, an estate-owner and his team of keepers could rely on fielding a private army of beaters. For example, in the time of the first Duke of Westminster's shooting at Eaton in Cheshire, the headkeeper was aided on shoot days not only by his team of twenty underkeepers, but also by eighty estate workers who acted as beaters, and who wore wide-brimmed, scarlet felt hats, white smocks, and wide, brown leather belts with heavy brass buckles. Modern keepers, faced with such a team, might be excused for panicking. They would not know what to do with them all! Line them out across a half-mile field or wood, and you would have a man every five paces. Such armies of beaters were organised with military precision, with platoons of stops, regiments of flankers, and brigades of beaters. They were old hands at the job, reliant on the estate, and under the close supervision of the keepers. They might ghost through a wood with no more sound than the constant tapping of sticks with crescendos here and there as they moved birds up to the flushing points.

Today, all that has changed. On an estate which once might have seen a hundred men, the single-handed keeper may now be struggling to raise fifteen. Things can be particularly difficult in areas that have a large number of Saturday shoots. Beaters pay is at such a low level that nobody, surely, can imagine that they turn out for the money. Good men with useful dogs are at a premium. If you have to cover the same ground with ten men as you once did with a hundred, then the gaps have to be plugged, and there is no better material for getting that job done than a team of controlled spaniels.

Many books written on the subject of gundogs have considered the subject of beaters' dogs purely and simply from the viewpoint of what the dog and his master should be putting in to the day. However, as this book is intended primarily for those who shoot over their own dogs, to whom any dalliances with the beating line may be of secondary importance, let us look, instead, at what they and their canine companions may get out of it!

What I am about to say may cause some raised eyebrows, perhaps even hackles, because I truly believe that the number of spaniels being used for beating, and beating alone, may have some long-term, adverse effects upon the breed. The point is that a spaniel's *raison d'être* is to find, flush, stand steady to the shot and fall of game, and then retrieve if necessary and, when any of those activities are denied, or made too easy, the dog's work is likely to suffer.

Many spaniel owners with greater experience and knowledge than myself, and a growing number of those involved in field trials, have been commenting upon the fact that many modern spaniels, while certainly *covering* their ground, are not seriously *hunting*. On a close scent, they should be coming to a sharp halt in their quartering, their noses going into overdrive and their tails accelerating into a blur of waving flag as they burrow into cover, out of which emerges a protesting pheasant or other quarry. It does not always happen. Indeed, there are many modern spaniels that show an aversion to cover, virtually refusing to bash a bramble or thrash a thorn. The suggestion, to me, is that these dogs have had it too easy. They have grown accustomed to working ground that is thick with birds, whereas the spaniel's character as a game-producer may only be honed to perfection where game is thin on the ground that the wee chap has learned that no opportunity is to be missed.

Then comes the shot, and so far as some spaniels are concerned, it seems almost unexpected. This is shown most clearly by the fact that they fail, time and again, to mark the fall of the game. Subsequently, if they have been trained to it, they may be handled by signals to the fall or, alternatively, wait for their handler to march up and point to the bird. In either case, there seems to be a failure to associate the flush of game with the probability of having something to retrieve. Of course, it might simply be that their owner is a lousy shot. But I suspect that it is most likely, in a great number of cases, to have arisen out of a dog's concentrated experience of the beating line where, quite simply, they seldom see the game shot.

EARLY WARNINGS

These are some of the considerations that you might like to take into account before taking your young spaniel into the beating line; a spaniel that you will also be looking to for sport when out rough shooting. Many will disagree, but I think that too many 'easy finds' and no shot immediately subsequent to the flush can take the edge off a spaniel's performance.

But there is another side to the coin. A keen, young dog can, in the midst of so much game, get 'steamed-up' and 'over-heated'. In other words, his nostrils are so full of scent that reason is set aside. He is drunk on scent. His hunting pattern falls apart because there is no longer any need for it, and soon the previously well-behaved dog is running riot. Let's face it, you have to sit hard on some spaniels to keep them hunting in proper range at the best of times, where game is thin but cover heavy. Try doing the same thing on the bare ground beneath an unbrashed conifer plantation, where you are bent double, and your dog can see fifty or more pheasants scuttling ahead. The demands of the beating line mean that it is virtually impossible to give a young spaniel your undivided attention. Once your grip on him is lost, he may be gone forever and your rough shooting days become a misery of trying to hold him within range. If you catch a young springer soon enough, you may pull him back from this loss of control, but the longer it continues, the harder it becomes to put things right. In the case of a cocker spaniel it is virtually impossible, I am told, to regain any control which has been lost. If I owned one of these delightful, hard working and clever little spaniels, I would think long and hard before entering him to the trials and tribulations of the beating line.

All this is quite contrary to what some gundogs books have had to say about beating. A number of writers have stated that, once your spaniel has reached a suitable level of training, he will gain greatly from working in the line of beaters on a driven shoot. They obviously regard the beating line as some sort of advanced training ground, encouraging the notion that your and your spaniel's reputation will spread quickly among the local keepers and, before long, you will be picking and choosing which shoots you wish to attend. It all sounds rather glorious. Soon, they suggest, you will also be invited to join in the picking-up.

Stop and think. This is all very well for those folk who are interested in dogs first and shooting second. It is also an excellent 'finishing ground' for professional trainers to give their 'money on paws' some experience of the shooting field before they are handed back to their owners, or advertised in the sporting press; 'one season's experience in the shooting field'. If, however, you want a spaniel that works as a spaniel – hunting, flushing, standing steady, marking and finally retrieving, is it wise to put your young dog into an environment where these actions are totally separated and may, indeed, become superfluous?

The required experience for a spaniel is not best sought on the driven shoot. But of course, if you do not intend to do much shooting over your own dogs, then you will feel fully justified in ignoring what I have to say.

PICKERS-UP

Leaving the beating line behind, let's move on to look at what is happening with the guns. Sticking with pheasants, the bread-and-butter of driven shooting, it is important, from the point of view of working with dogs, to realise that we live in an age in which the accent is, or should be, firmly fixed on quality, rather than quantity. Allied to this should be the realisation that many sporting writers over the past decade have been preaching the philosophy of open chokes and small shot. Put these two factors together – high birds and what *may* be inadequate armoury – and the result is many failures to kill cleanly.

If you will not take my word for it, talk to those who regularly pick-up on quality shoots that take paying guests. Guns may believe that a bird has been missed when, in fact, it has been hit with insufficient pellets of inadequate striking energy in order to ensure a kill. On some shoots, from positions which may be 200yd behind the guns, the pickers-up will soon be able to suggest who is firing 1oz of 7 shot through true cylinder barrels, and those who are firing $1\frac{1}{16}$ oz of 6 or 7 through three-quarter or full chokes. Given the required circumstances, two or three pickers-up with well-trained, experienced retrievers may account for twenty or even thirty per cent of the bag. This can lead to arguments and worse at the end of the day on a commercially let shoot, where the team of guns insist that they have only 160 birds, but there are nearly 200 in the game cart!

Sticking with these suggested percentages, this leads to the realisation that perhaps 65-75 per cent of the bag are killed 'clean', and fall close to the line of guns, that 20-30 per cent carry on some for distance and are subsequently gathered by the pickers-up if they are employed and positioned correctly; and that even on the best ordered shoots, perhaps 5 per cent will escape either to recover, or become a fox's supper.

Taking the case of an 'average' shoot, where 120 pheasants may be shot during the course of six drives, this means 20 birds shot per drive. Of these, we might expect that fourteen or fifteen will fall close to the guns, four or five will be gathered by pickers-up stationed some distance behind the line and, unless the pick-up is particularly efficient, one pheasant will be left ungathered. I would emphasise that these figures are purely for the purposes of illustration.

If pickers-up had not been employed, the bag might have been as little as 90, rather than the 120 obtained. Beside purely humanitarian considerations which should be first and foremost in the minds of anybody who likes to call himself a sportsman, birds that are left unpicked represent a loss of potential income to the shoot. At today's prices for pheasants, an extra dozen brace for the game dealer will justify the employment of a pair of pickers-up with their retrievers on any shoot of this scale. And on a commercial shoot, the arithmetic of picker-up accountancy becomes even more arresting. With travelling syndicates at the time of writing paying between £15 and £20 for each pheasant shot; and sometimes more; the employment of pickers-up will have increased the shoot income by up to £500. I will not bore you with detailing the figures on those commercial shoots where bags of 240, 360, 480 and more pheasants are shot in a day. In such cases, the employment of pickers-up makes good financial sense, as well as being a moral necessity.

Pickers-up who continually insist on standing up with the guns, for all the world as if they are out to spectate and enjoy themselves, are little more than a waste of time, effort, and birds. The job has to be done properly. And, when it is, it provides an ideal training and working environment for retrievers, both young and old.

Picking-up, unlike beating, tends to be a solitary affair. A picker-up is required to get on quietly with his work, with minimum fuss and need for supervision. It has to be said that this can be quite daunting for a newcomer to a shoot. The keeper may have been held up in conversation with the guns and the beater's wagon is loaded up and ready to go to the next drive. There *you* are, struggling through a spruce wood in search of a runner that one of the guns insists he has down. Things can get a little confusing, particularly if, in the heat of the moment, you have been forgotten about or left without transport. You may have little or no idea as to where the next drive is being staged! Hopefully, you will have been put in the care of the old boy who drives the game cart, or a fellow-picker-up who knows his way about.

Keep your wits about you, at all times. As an example of what can happen by placing yourself in the wrong place at the wrong time, let me recount the tale of a field trial at which I had been invited to shoot. It was the first drive, a mix of pheasants and partridges, with the partridges just skimming over the hedge to our front before exploding like bursts of shrapnel at the sight of the waiting guns, retrievers, handlers, judges and stewards. I was next to the right-hand flank gun, and we had been asked to drop our birds either right onto the line, or into a patch of cover some 30 yards behind. Perhaps we were both a little bit embarrassed at having brought about the elimination of two fine looking young Labradors that had shown the termerity, in the judge's eye, of showing their unsteadiness by taking one pace each towards birds that had virtually fallen on their heads with a bounce and much fluttering of wings. So as the next covey came through and over us, we both raised our barrels and turned in unison to drop them behind. We both shouted a warning. Standing there, barely 50 yards behind, was an elderly lady with an equally elderly black Labrador sitting at heel and watching the proceedings. Something runs cold in the pit of your stomach at such times.

It turned out that she was a competitor who had arrived late at the meeting place. Hearing the sound of gunfire, she had followed it as best she could, thinking that, as long as she came up quietly, under cover of a high hedge, it would be perfectly acceptable for her to stand and watch. In fact, she seemed more than a little bit irritated at a judge who suggested otherwise.

We walked away, leaving her arguing with the judges and steward, assuming that she would be sent for the field-trialler's equivalent of an early shower. However, there she was, at the next drive, putting her old dog through its paces as if nothing had happened.

When I had a small word with the 'powers-that-be' later in the day, they shuffled their feet rather nervously and I got the distinct impression that they were either fearful of risking the wrath of this awesome creature, or perhaps that of her connections. They actually insisted that she was very knowledgeable, and picked-up regularly on shoots in her area. I can only assume that she had lived in that area since she was a girl, since when she had been wheeled from shoot to shoot ensconced in Husky, tweed skirt and brogues, to be seated on a large shooting stick alongside her husband's friends, nephews, cousins, brothers or whoever else might have drawn the short straw that day.

PICKING-UP

But let us get back to picking-up with the presumption that you and your young dog are new to the job, for, if you are not, you will hardly need any advice from me. And let me assume, for this first drive, that you have found yourself a good vantage point, perhaps 100yd behind the line of guns. The distance should seldom be less. You will, of course, have ascertained where you can send your dog. Perhaps the bird are being fed into the wood immediately behind you, from which they will be flushed for the

An old-hand at the picking-up of game in Hampshire.

next drive. Your dog, if sent in to search for a runner, might flush some of these birds and thus ruin the drive, so keep him out. Such birds which have fallen in the wood should subsequently be picked by the beaters' dogs.

Settle yourself down with your dog. Stoke your pipe if you wish, or unwrap a sweetie, but do not take out the morning paper and settle down for a bit of a read. From the moment the first shot is fired, your attention should be devoted to the birds coming over the guns to your front. Watch for those birds that show some sign of being hit, but keep coming on. You may see one jerk as the shot is fired or the bird might have a leg hanging; it may be one of a dozen things and, with a little experience, you will find yourself *knowing* a bird is hit, without being able to say why. Watch the bird down. An untidy landing is a sign of a hit bird. Sometimes birds will fly on without showing any evidence of being hit and then, far behind the line, crumple into a tumbling ball of feathers.

In an ideal world you would, of course, keep your dog sitting firmly at heel until the drive is over. You will see this as first rate steadiness training for your dog. However, in the real world, when time may be at a premium, and a runner is going down, you may decide to give it only enough time to get to cover, before setting off after it with your dog. At the same time, you will have to keep an eye on other birds that may be streaming over from the line of guns. Remember that while a bird in the hand is worth two in the bush, if you remember the bushes where the other two fall you may well end up with three in the hand, and everybody will be happy. And all the time, you and your dog are learning, and you are building on those foundations of initial training that should develop your dog into an ideal working and shooting companion.

The building of the dog's experience will manifest itself on those occasions when your good dog knows that a bird is hit, but you do not. I wrote earlier of developing a sense for knowing when a bird is hit, without being able to say why. This is true, but an experienced dog can take this recognition to a much higher peak of achievement. It seems that they quickly learn to recognise flight abnormalities.

At a shoot least season, I was placed in a woodland ride some distance behind and out of sight of the guns. Neither I, nor my dogs, could see the birds as they crossed the line and so were unable to judge how they reacted to the shots fired. As the birds came over us, planing on set wings, they all looked the same to me. But I noted that my elder-statesman Labrador was giving them all the once-over. Some he would just glance at. Others held his gaze until they had passed behind us and out of sight.

I would have said that none of those birds was hit but, at the end of the drive, I sent him back, while keeping my younger dog at heel. The old boy came back with one, two, three, four pheasants in quick succession.

Standing as far back from the line as possible, and reasonable, gives the picker-up and his dogs a far better chance of marking hit birds. If you are much closer than 100yd behind, you will be forever finding yourself turning to mark down uncertainties. In such cases, being unable to look in two places at once, you may miss a hit bird in front of you. And do remember, so far as possible, to stand still and wear drab clothing and a hat or cap to shield your face. A wounded pheasant will glide down if it has not noticed you, but summon up a last burst of energy that will carry it away beyond if you are moving about, or standing in the open and wearing bright clothes.

A final word on picking-up. If you want to stay popular wth those guns who are attended by their own dogs, remember that they may be keen to give these dogs a few retrieves of their own. Stay back and pick only the long range birds, or position yourself behind a dogless gun who will welcome your assistance.

IN THE SHOOTING LINE

Those birds that fall close to the guns should really be gathered by the guns themselves although, on a commercial shoot, the organiser or the keeper will ensure that the ground is fairly well swept, either by a picker-up placed with the guns for that purpose, or by one or two of the beaters with reliable dogs. Good beaters with dogs are normally more than happy to help out with picking-up, rather than leaning on their sticks and chin-wagging.

What is required of a dog for this short-range, picking-up work? The answer may be, if a dog is to do the job well, that it may need rather more polish, certainly as far as steadiness is concerned, than the dog used by a picker-up well behind the line.

The Field Trail where a couple of young Labradors were eliminated for taking a pace, hardly more than a shuffle, towards partridges that were dropping almost on their heads serves as a good example. Some may see this as taking the search for perfection to unreasonable extremes, but it serves as a pointer to what is required. If either of those dogs had been with a gun whose attention was on his shooting, rather than under the close control of a handler who was giving the dog his full attention, the 'shuffle' could easily have developed into a full-blown run-in. With a few of those under his belt, the dog's steadiness would be in tatters.

The high point of a retriever's behaviour might be seen during the course of a productive drive where birds are raining down fast and furious on all sides, and the dog does nothing but turn his head to mark each fall. This level of steadiness is an outright compliment to the dog's training while his ability to carry out difficult retrieves with dash and style comes from within himself, plus the experience he has been given. To me, there are few finer spectacles than a brace or trio of worldly-wise Labradors displaying their rock-steadiness throughout the course of a drive without a second glance from their shooting owner, and then seeing the same dogs dashing out when permit has been given; lifting each and every bird, being called off their neighbour's without a hint of protest or jealousy; getting the job done with maximum efficiency in minimum time. But you can't expect this sort of behaviour straight off the training field.

How rarely such paragons of virtue are seen. The problems are fairly obvious. Let me offer a scenario.

RISKING RUIN

A businessman, who has taken up shooting in middle age, has seen dogs working on the shoot where he is a syndicate member and he has decided that he would like a dog for himself. He does realise, however, that he has very little idea of what is entailed in the training of a retriever and, because he is a busy man, he does not have the time to undertake such an endeavour. So he decides to buy a trained dog. He scans the shooting press, or hears by word of mouth that a black Labrador with two season's experience is for sale, and he decides to pay the not inconsiderable price asked.

This deal might be struck in, say, March. The trainer tells the businessman that the dog is house trained, and so the new dog is allowed in the house, with the family, who were promised that it would be their pet as well as the father's shooting companion. The father insists that he will feed the dog and, at weekends, he may take it for a long walk. On these walks, he may well throw a dummy for the dog. It seems both unnecessary and unfair to expect the dog to walk at heel on these outings, or to make him wait too long, if at all, before making his retrieves. After all, the kids do not expect him to wait for the ball that they have thrown for him in the garden. Need I say more? The dog has already been ruined.

If, on the other hand, the dog had been kennelled and, instead of worrying about who fed it, the owner got himself out of bed twenty minutes earlier to give the dog a walk, mainly at heel, and set aside an hour each weekend for a proper 'training' session in which retrieving was seen more as an exercise in steadiness, rather than a repetitive bit of jollification, then the dog, when the shooting season came around, would have been in with a fighting chance.

That chance would have been greatly improved if, for at least the first few shoots, the dog's owner had set aside his gun, stood in the line, and given the dog his undivided attention. There really is no getting away from the old adage, 'train in haste, repent at leisure'.

The result of not giving enough attention to your dog's steadiness is that he is soon running-in to the fall of birds, tearing about during the drive to the consternation of your fellow guns and, generally, making a damned nuisance of himself. This, at least, can be cured by putting the dog on a tethered lead. Nothing wrong with that. Many dogs live a dual life as family pets first, and shooting companions second. And if they spend only ten days out of 365 in the shooting field, you can hardly expect them to avoid falling foul of temptation. It is what happens at the end of the drive, when the birds are to be gathered, which should decide whether or not a dog deserves the title of gundog, and the dog's performance is a clear reflection of the thought, as well as effort, put into its initial training. After an early interest in retrieving has been established, the dog should no longer be sent to retrieve dummies that are lying in plain view. To carry on with such 'easy' retrieves would encourage the dog to rely on his eyes, and ignore his nose. This practice should be carried on to the shooting field and, certainly in a dog's first season, he should not be sent for birds lying in clear view. Only a very lazy owner will not walk 10yd to pick up such a bird himself.

Quality dog work is not, necessarily, a product of the quantity of experience. Consider those smaller shoots, where perhaps fifty driven birds fall in a day, and the guns feel that the

The rough-shooter's spaniel will also accompany its owner at more formal events.

services of a picker-up are not justified. In such situations, the guns need really good dogs and the patience to let them complete their tasks. A dog whose only experience is of picking up easy retrieves at 20yd range on short-cropped grass is hardly likely to shine in such company.

It is only human to allow sentiment to influence our decision on whether or not to take along old Fido. Many owners like to bring their dog to the shoot and even the most incompetent dog, unless he interferes with other's enjoyment, should not raise any objections. But, surely, it is far better to make that small effort throughout the year which is enough to ensure that we have a dog that is capable of doing a job of work on the day.

There remains the question as to which breed of gundog is most likely to 'get the job done' most successfully. One immediately thinks of the Labrador for those who enjoy regular sport on the driven shoot. However, many spaniels are seen sitting alongside their masters at pegs on the pheasant shoots, and in butts on the moor. There is nothing new in this. Reference was made in an earlier chapter to a letter written by Sir Frederick Millbank to *Shooting* magazine in September, 1888.

> I have always used spaniels that retrieve well – I find they
> are twice as quick as the large retriever . . .

and Sir Frederick continued this them of speed in the pick-up by stating:

> It is a great advantage to have your birds picked as quickly
> as possible, and then off to another drive.

One hundred years later, nothing has changed. In fact, if anything, there seems to be ever more hustle and bustle to be on to the next drive. Sometimes, it may seem that the sound of the last shot fired has hardly faded before somebody is shouting 'Guns this way, please'. And so, yes, speed in the pick-up, so far as those birds that fall close to the guns are concerned, will be seen as a great advantage on many shoots.

RETRIEVING SPANIELS?

But spaniels operating in a pure retrieving role? I have just been criticising the use of spaniels in a purely flushing role, as beaters' dogs. Do the same criticisms apply to this alternative use of spaniels?

In my experience with my own dogs, whereas prolonged experience of hunting an over-abundance of game, that the spaniel does not see shot, is likely to be detrimental to his hunting pattern, dedication and steadiness, picking-up experience serves only to heighten a spaniel's retrieving ability, and perhaps improve its steadiness. While I certainly would not advise the driven-shooting-only man to dash off and buy a spaniel, if he also does some rough shooting, and has a spaniel to accompany him on these forays, then the selfsame dog may happily accompany him to driven shoots; so long as it is of the right type. 'The right type' of dog is one which has had some extra attention given to bringing out its retrieving ability and ensuring that it is steady not only to the fall of game shot over it, but also through the course of a drive. There is a difference between expecting a spaniel to pause briefly after it has flushed a bird which has been shot, before sending the dog out to retrieve, and expecting it to sit for half-an-hour or more while pheasants rain down. By their very nature, spaniels are very different to the stolid Labrador. The sight of falling game is likely to get them steamed-up. It is perhaps best to err on the side of caution, expect the worst, and tether.

In extreme cases, the spaniel will express its excitement by whimpering and whining. This can also happen, of course, in the case of excitable young retrievers. Nip it in the bud before you have a dog that whines constantly and loudly, to the irritation of your fellow guns. If a gruff voice is not sufficient, I am afraid that this is one of those situations where a quick smack on the dog's rump, or cut with the lead, may be required – short, sharp, shock treatment.

Spaniels, then, can be useful, working companions both for guns and pickers-up alike, particularly in those situations where a large number of birds are known to be down in a given area of cover, but none of them has been marked accurately. It might be said that the spaniel, with a good, close quartering pattern, can excel at this style of short-range retrieving. A specialist Retriever breed, on the other hand, will show up all but a few spaniels where more difficult, long-range retrieves are required. My money would be on the spaniels to pick-up the birds that fall close to the guns in minimum time but, if there was a bird two fields back, the retriever should score every time. It is these rather different requirements, incidentally, that lead so many serious pickers-up to work with both spaniels and retrievers, simultaneously.

A woodcock in the hand on the Isle of Skye.

70

CHAPTER FOUR

Snipe and Woodcock

It is possible to divide shooters into two 'types'. Which particular type an individual falls into may not be revealed until he finds himself with two shooting invitations or opportunities on the same date. One involves the near certainty of a hundred or more driven pheasants. The other is for the uncertainties of a day's snipe or 'cock shooting where the bag might be ten, twenty or none at all. Which invitation would you accept?

Another time when it is possible to distinguish the two types is when an individual is given the choice of a right-and-left at a pheasant and a woodcock. All other things being equal, a great deal is revealed by which mark the individual's barrels swing to first.

I can only say that I would accept the day's snipe or 'cock shooting and, without a doubt, with a pheasant and a 'cock in the air at the same time, the pheasant would have to wait. If, on the other hand, we had been talking of a snipe and a teal, flushed at the very same moment from the reed-covered marshy shore of a jewelled lochan set high in the hills, or from that over grown ditch, it would have to be first come, first served.

I count my blessings to have experienced days similar to the style of sport enjoyed by Charles St. John, described earlier, when snipe, woodcock, grouse and duck all figured in the bag. Not only are the essential characters of such species so attractive but so are the wild places where we seek them out. And, as important is the company of like-minded sportsmen.

71

Some would suggest that the dedicated snipe and woodcock men are a race apart. That may be true. Whatever the case, they are often among the keenest and most appreciative of dog-owners and fanciers. Before the dogs and the shooting, however, let me take a closer look at the birds themselves.

SNIPE

I have said that we seek out snipe and 'cock among the wild places. This does not change the fact, however, that snipe can be found around sewage farms on the outskirts of industrialised towns and cities, nor that, on occasion, a 'cock may be flushed from the rhododendrons in a municipal park. Both of these species can be extremely unpredictable, and there is seldom room for such words as 'always' or 'never' in any description of them.

The snipe is best described, perhaps, as having the appearance of a small wader. Snipe are both resident and migratory in our islands. The sportsman's interest is in the common snipe which weighs about 4-5oz, and has fourteen tail feathers. Other species of snipe encountered in Britain are the tiny jack snipe, weighing only about 2oz and having twelve tail feathers, and the great snipe weighing 8oz with sixteen tail feathers.

Incidentally, I include the number of tail feathers as a surer identification point than weight alone. For, while 4oz is certainly the most common size, much larger specimens of common snipe have been recorded. I have seen snipe to 6oz, and J.E. Harting in his *Handbook of British Birds* records that in 1891 he received three specimens from Dingwall, Lerwick, which had been shot a few days previously but still weighed 5¾oz, 6¼oz and 6¾oz respectively.

The snipe's long bill is extemely sensitive. They feed normally on undrained marshes, by pools, shallows or anywhere which provides soft ground into which it can thrust its bill in order to secure food. It will, incidentally, feed by both day and night as opposed to the woodcock which appears entirely nocturnal in this respect.

The sportsman's study of the snipe is closely tied to the wind and weather. If frost comes to the ground, the snipe can no longer feed and soon depart. This, of course, is why the milder, wetter west coast is so well-favoured in harsh winters. The wind has a serious part to play in deciding how best to come to terms with this sporting little target.

THE GUN FOR SNIPE

Patsy O'Halloran was a professional snipe shooter of Kilkee, in County Clare. He is also widely accepted as having been among the very finest of performers on this testing species. Tales are still told of how he would wait until he judged two fast departing snipe to be in line, and then snap them down with one shot. He performed with a graceful style, with a quick and unhurried action, and perfect co-ordination of eye, hand, body and feet; and he was quite murder on the snipe. In a shooting career that spanned fifty years, he bagged 45,000 snipe, exceeding 2,000 during the harsh winter of 1880-81. His best day produced 46 snipe and 13 woodcock.

For the last 25 years of his shooting career, O'Halloran, who it can be safely assumed knew as much about snipe shooting as anyone, chose a hammerless 12-bore gun with 28in barrels, bored cylinder and half choke, weighing 6½lb. This is, in fact, a standard game gun, ideally suited to all forms of walked-up sport, and shooting over dogs, and denies the need for any sort of specialist gun for snipe. O'Halloran did, however, choose a rather special cartridge. He recognised the value of a really dense pattern to hit the tiny, 4oz target, and got this by loading his cartridges with 1⅛oz of No.9 shot. His results speak for themselves. Despite recent changes in permitted loads for clay pigeon shooting, such cartridges are widely available still in the 'Skeet' option although, personally, I would probably settle for the slightly thinner pattern but greater striking energy of No.8 shot, just in case a spring of teal had settled on the marsh.

SNIPE SHOOTING AND DOGS

For those who prefer to shoot this way, some of the formalities of the driven day can be introduced into snipe shooting. On a small marsh, a couple of beaters, or a solitary man, is often sufficient to flush the snipe toward the waiting guns. Spaniels may be used to flush the birds, but the best day's snipe driving that I ever enjoyed was produced by a keeper walking towards our hidden positions and striking a tin plate with a wooden spoon! The wind direction is a decisive factor in choosing the drive, but no more so than a previous knowledge of the snipe's favoured exit routes from the marsh.

Dogs are not required until the drive is over, when they are presented with a real challenge in finding perhaps as many as a dozen tiny snipe spread over what may be a fairly large area of tussocky ground. Retrievers whose knowledge is limited to picking-up on pheasant shoots may find the challenge beyond them, but they will learn.

The experience of E.C. Keith of Swanton Morely House in Norfolk when he adopted the practice of driving snipe on a bog of about 40 acres seems to prove the point. In the season of 1925-26, before driving was introduced, he shot 17 snipe off the bog. The next season's driving produced 156, and the following season 410, due not only to the fact that snipe conditions had been improved by the local river oveflowing its banks, but also because the local dogs were gaining in experience at gathering the slain.

The same can be said of the experiences of H.L. Horsfall of Dunwich in Suffolk, where extensive marshes run along the seashore. Snipe were only shot as an aside, at the end of a day's covert shooting, and the average bag for the season was normally about 40 until 1923 when driving was introduced, the marsh mapped out into beats, the snipe's flights studied, and butts erected. From then on, the following seasons produced 159, 164 and 359 snipe. It was admitted that, to begin with, many shot birds were not picked but that after a while, and with careful 'training' of dogs, these losses became comparatively few. Now, I would argue that you cannot really 'train' a dog to snipe, so much as offer them plenty of experience upon which to develop, but that may seem to be splitting hairs.

It may not be the snipe's lack of size or scent that causes problems among dogs unentered to the species. It seems rather that the dog may at first seem not to associate the scent with something to be hunted, flushed or picked. Indeed, some dogs seem initially to find the scent of a snipe distasteful. My small springer spaniel, Drummer, caused me great amusement on his first few snipe. He would pick them up gingerly, often by a wing-tip, and carry them to me, after some coaxing, with his top lip curled back in obvious disgust. And here was a dog named in recognition of my affection for snipe! But he soon sorted himself out, and today, if he could speak, I think he would tell me that a day on the snipe bog is one of his favourite things.

Pointers and setters may have much the same reaction to snipe scent. Inexperienced pointers may seem next to useless on their first outings on the snipe grounds, and then, suddenly, as if the penny has dropped, the merest puff of snipe scent galvanises them into action, or rather turns them to stone. I noticed this at a field trial for pointers and setters held on a Scottish moor, but well attended by teams of Irishmen with their dogs. The trial was held in early August because, provided a shot is fired when the birds are put up, no birds need be killed over these breeds. Their ability is concerned purely with game-finding. Anyway, enough snipe were still on the moor at this early date to reveal that many of the Irish dogs had had plenty of experience on them, and that an individual might be so intense on snipe that the same dog looked almost casual on grouse. Perhaps snipe should be seen as an acquired taste with some dogs, but once the taste *is* acquired, they can't get enough of it.

An Irish friend of mine is a specialist 'cock and snipe shot who performs shooting miracles on the bog, and he always shoots over a pointer. With the dog on point, the man can choose his position to a certain extent, and he normally chooses to come up on the left flank of his dog before encouraging her forward to flush the quarry. His choice of pointer is rather interesting, I think. We had been enjoying a great morning of grouse shooting over pointers on 12 August, on a good dogging moor in the Scottish Highlands. Over the lunch of sandwiches and beer, I listened to a mellow duet of western voices in deep conservation about dogs and their ways, training, handling and so on. One particular bitch had caught my friend's eye, perhaps after giving him a chance to prove himself at a 'walke of snytes'. The keeper then mentioned that this would probably be the bitch's last season because her pace was losing its edge and he was bringing on some fine pups.

A deal was struck and, when the grouse shooting came to a halt, my friend returned to collect his new shooting companion. One month later, she was adjudged ready to make the transition from moor to bog. By Christmas she was getting into the new way of things and, soon after, my friend knew he had something very special.

The bitch seemed to appreciate that she could set her own pace in front of a man who would take time in reloading and who would give her a rest, whenever she needed it, while he sat to stoke and smoke his pipe. And she learned, when she had the wind of a snipe, to approach it like a heron stalking a frog, rather than a charging water buffalo that would clear a marsh as quickly as Major Yeates's Maria.

It is every bit as enjoyable, I have found, to shoot snipe over pointers or setters, as it is to shoot grouse over the same breeds. And very much the same rules apply that we should drive where populations are concentrated, but dog over larger areas where they are scattered. The alternative, of course, is walking up with or without spaniels. Without a spaniel, or a hunter-pointer-retriever, you will need a good retriever walking to heel to gather any slain.

As stated earlier, the weather and wind in particular has an influence on the way that we should conduct our sport. Snipe will feed at night, particularly under the moon, but a wild and stormy night will upset them, the following day finding them still on the feeding grounds; very alert, difficult to approach and, therefore, hard to shoot. After a fine feeding night, however, they will settle down with full stomachs to doze the day away on heather or bracken clad hillsides, fields and the like, rather than on the undrained marsh where they have fed. Some shooting men do not seem to realise this aspect of their resting behaviour, as witnessed by comments such as, 'Imagine finding a snipe in this unlikely spot. What could it have been feeding upon?' to which the knowledgeable reply is, 'It was not feeding; only resting'. Snipe will often show their preference for a dry bed, rather than the damp couches of the bog and marsh.

Having found your snipe, and flushed it, what then makes it such a difficult target is the manner of its departure flight. Nothing could have been better designed to throw off a following hawk, or shotgun barrel. The snipe rises with its distinctive 'scarp, scarp' cry of alarm and, as soon as it is clear of the ground, it zigs, darts, dodges, twists, swerves and zags away over its first 20 or 30yd of ground. Try shooting that in copybook style!

Some old hands tease newcomers to the snipe bog by telling them that they must always shoot snipe as they zig, rather than zag. More serious discussions are centred around whether the snipe should be shot immediately that it rises, or given time to settle down into a more straightforward flight pattern. The answer is that both are right, depending upon the circumstances.

On days when the snipe are alert, and still feeding on the marsh, you will find yourself tempted to order your dog to heel as bird after bird flushes at near maximum range, or beyond it. Even those birds that rise at about 25yd will still be zigging and zagging as they pass the 50yd marker, and you have nothing to lose in getting your gun up as quickly as possible and taking a snap shot.

If, on the other hand, the birds are found away from the wettest areas, are obviously well fed, dozing as you approach, and letting you get close, then you may well choose to let them carry on through their zigging and zagging, then try to knock them down when they are 30 to 40yd out; virtually at the same range at which the more alert birds were springing.

Beside the question of when to shoot your snipe, there are those hoary old arguments about whether it is better to walk up or down-wind. Besides the fact that dogs, be they pointers, setters or spaniels, will do best when working into the wind, there are other matters to be taken into consideration. Matters that might tempt you to leave all but a close, heel-keeping dog at home.

The upwind approach seems ideally suited not only to your dogs, but also to those days when there is a strong, blustery wind blowing which, besides covering your approach, infers that the birds will not have fed well on the previous night and will, therefore, be on the alert. On the other hand, there are many experienced snipe-shooters who argue for the downwind approach on the basis that, as the birds normally rise into the wind, this gives you more time to sort out your footing and get off your shot. And others argue for a cross-wind approach . . .

At the end of the day, such arguments may help to pass the time when snipe-shooters gather together but, unless you are shooting a series of small, separated marshes, to be shot in turn, they may be seen as more theoretical than practical. After all, what goes up must come down, just as the bog-trotting snipe man who sets off up-wind from base must return it down-wind, and will probably indulge in some cross-wind walking inbetween, so as not to cover the same ground twice.

SNIPE BAGS AND GROUNDS

A discussion of the deeds and bags of professional shooters such as Patsy O'Halloran, and some bags of snipe shot by driving in East Anglia tends, as I have explained elsewhere, to seem distasteful in the modern age. We prefer to think in terms of quality rather than quantity. However, bags of totally wild species when used for comparative purposes can be seen as important pointers from which to judge the species' current status.

Snipe are still plentiful in our islands, make no mistake about that. Nevertheless, their numbers have been significantly reduced. This is a reflection of man's high-handed attitude toward his environment and the other species that inhabit the earth. And by 'man', I mean the politician, industrialist, farmer and forester. All these groups have great power bases of influence in society, and a popular media that can easily be manipulated in the case of such sensitive issues as shooting. But the sportsman has never threatened the snipe, or the woodcock for that matter. Any person or organisation who suggests otherwise is just looking for a convenient scapegoat. The sportsman yearns for times past when every field had its undrained corners and patches where it was common to flush a snipe or two, and there were marshes and bogs throughout our lands where large populations of these little birds could thrive. It is the property speculator, industrialist and, above all, the farmers and foresters, with the damnable drainage work and thoughtless planting, aided and abetted by lobby-inspired grants and incentives, who seem incapable of seeing a wilderness area without sticking in

Where moor meets marsh, snipe may be added to the grouse-shooter's bag.

their dirty boots, diggers, mole ploughs, bulldozers and whatever else it takes to bring the area into what they call 'productivity'. To twist an old phrase, 'They create a desert, and call it progress'. Leaving this politicising aside, let me offer some suggestions as to the numbers of snipe there might have been in the past.

Some of my paternal grandmother's family farmed on Tiree in the Inner Hebrides, where their land and the climate were ideally suited to producing early crops for the mainland's fruit and vegetable markets. In winter, the same lands provided an ideal environment for snipe, and it was on Tiree that the largest bag of snipe to which anyone has admitted was shot. Lord Elphinstone and J.D. Cobbold shot 1,108 snipe between 25 October and 3 November, 1906, accounting for 249 on 29 October. In later years, J.D. Cobbold was able to shoot 151 snipe to his own gun on 30 January, 1915. This is, I believe, still the individual British record for a day's snipe shooting, followed by a bag of 105 shot by the Hon. E. de Moleyns at Dingle, County Kerry, in 1867.

In January 1891, Colonel Richard Denny shot 273 snipe in seven days, his best day's total being 65, in County Kerry. And in the season of 1846-7, a keeper on Lord Sligo's estate near Westport bagged the mind-boggling total of 3,330 snipe.

Moving back to the Hebrides, although Islay is perhaps best known for its woodcock and malt whiskies, it has also produced some outstanding bags of snipe. In the seasons between 1924 and 1928, bags of 790, 511, 880 and 641 were reported, with two guns in the first season, and three thereafter.

Those acquainted with the snipe grounds of the Scottish Highlands and Hebrides, or the sporting scene in the west of Ireland, will know that much of these grounds are rolling miles of country, and often have little immediately obvious signs of the hand of man. Unless you are capable of quite long and perhaps fairly strenuous exercise, you will not be able to make the most of the sport on offer. It is not simply a case of dragging yourself across the landscape. Quick decisions fill the bag, and clever footwork is not easy when one wader-clad leg is knee deep in bog-glar. Bog-trotting is the general rule, with excursions into rough heather and birch scrub to add woodcock to the tally; teal from the lochan and grouse from the hill. But what better way to end a day than with the dogs dried, fed and kennelled, the guns cleaned, tweeds steaming and reeking over the Aga, and a relaxing deep, hot bath with nothing but a dram and thoughts of a welcome dinner, as you recall each and every detail of your day in the wilds?

WOODCOCK

A woodcock in the hand might be said to look like an overgrown snipe. Overgrown in that the snipe will only weigh 4½oz whereas an average 'cock will weigh 12oz, and an occasional 'pounder' specimen has been recorded. This almost puts the 'cock into the same weight and size category as partridge, teal, and the like.

Many of the 'cock encountered on British shoots are migrants that come to our islands from late October onwards. The greatest numbers arrive on our shores from northern Europe at the time of the 'woodcock moon' − the first full moon in November which, presumably, serves to light their way. The wind direction also plays its part, with an easterly being the most favoured. The severity of the coming winter will then decide what proportion of the expanded national 'cock population remain spread across the country. Harsh mainland weather will drive extraordinary concentrations of 'cock to the softer west, from the Hebrides down through Galloway, west Wales, Cornwall, the Scilly Isles, and the west of Ireland.

The woodcock remains a mysterious bird. Modern game biologists may, if they are honest, admit that the sum of what they know about woodcock is still heavily outweighed by the details of what they do not. And even what they do know may be doubted by some folk. Woodcock have that effect on people. To offer just one example, there is the age-old debate about whether or not woodcock will carry their young . . . It was a fine, late afternoon on Speyside as I made my way down to the river with a salmon rod over my shoulder. My path led me through a typically thin, scrub birch wood, floored with tussocky grasses, brackens, ferns and the wild flowers of spring. A woodcock sprang at my feet. Seconds later, another followed, except that its flight seemed more laborious, as if it had just been tucking into a heavy meal. As it banked around a tree, I could clearly see that it had a chick gripped between its thighs. I was so close as to be able to see the chick's tiny eye.

When I wrote about this sighting in a sporting magazine of which I was then editor, more than a few readers suggested that I should have my eyes tested. When I pointed out that I still had a pilot's vision, they quipped that the problem might be with my brain, rather than my eyes. Two sporting gentlemen were prepared to say to my face that I was a liar! When I pointed to the accounts of the many naturalists and sportsmen who had witnessed this event, they were also labelled as liars. The whole thing reminded me of men who had never moved out of the parish in which they were born, refusing to believe that the earth was not flat. Those who called men who claimed to have sailed round the globe liars, or worse, and clung to their maps whose margins were etched with the words 'Beyond here, there be dragons . . .'.

But what nobody, surely, will argue about is that the woodcock is one of our most attractive quarry species, and among the most highly prized.

WOODCOCK SHOOTING AND DOGS

A gun that serves you for snipe, will serve you for woodcock. In other words, the standard, double-barrelled, hammerless

12-bore. As to cartridges, traditionalists would argue for a standard load of No.7 shot; perhaps a 1oz load for its excellent patterning, but a growing number of 'modernists' are showing a preference for No.8 shot, particularly for use in guns with open chokes, as often advised for driven game shooting.

As an alternative, there are those who argue for a lightweight gun, perhaps with short barrels to make it 'handy' for use in woodlands. I have sympathy with this attitude. For the last few seasons, I have done a lot of my woodcock and general rough shooting with a 20-bore over-and-under, with 26in barrels and weighing 6lb which can be seen as the minimum for keeping recoil to an acceptable level when using 1oz loads of No.7½ shot. With a single selective trigger, this gun fulfils many of my needs from pheasants to smaller game.

Turning to dogs, mention woodcocks to most shooting folk and they think of spaniels. Indeed, cocker spaniels were so named because, traditionally, they were used to flush 'cock for the sportsman. Nowadays, sadly, the cocker spaniel has lost much of the favour that it once enjoyed in shooting cirlces. Horses for courses, however, and springer spaniels have proved themselves quite superb for this class of work.

Having described the springer as superb, it is necessary to admit to some immediate reservations. Nothing has changed since the days when Colonel Hawker wrote that there was nothing better than a well trained spaniel for this class of work but that nine out of ten that he saw in the shooting field were quite useless. In fact, a badly trained, unruly spaniel is worse than useless. I can think of no worse fate than to find myself sandwiched between the antics of two unruly brutes that are 'doing their own thing' 50yd or more in front of the line. And you just know that while you may get away with suggesting virtually anything you can think of in regard to your neighbour's children, wife or mother, if you utter so much as a word of criticism about his spaniel, you will have made an enemy for life.

But I am getting ahead of myself. Let me introduce a note of formality to this consideration of 'cock shooting, by describing the class of sport that we enjoyed in Cornwall, and the type of driven shooting that has produced some of the legendary places and names of 'cock shooting.

This is not the place to go into a description of the laying-out and management of 'cock shoots. Suffice to say, I hope, that a woodcock covert should have a windproof perimeter and, again to keep out the draughts, be planted on irregular ground. Woodcock need plenty of 'edge' and this is achieved with low cover species, rides, gaps and glades. In such an ideal covert, I would prefer it if the beaters left their dogs at home. Equally, I would prefer to see half-a-dozen old, seasoned countrymen to flush the birds quietly, than a dozen yapping youngsters.

There again, how often do we see coverts laid out entirely with a view to harbouring and showing 'cock? And often your best beaters will only turn out for the opportunity to work their dogs. So, it is swings and roundabouts and, certainly where your coverts are extensive, a team of good men with staunch spaniels that will hunt the ground with the accent on quiet efficiency, rather than irrepressible energy, provide a near ideal solution to flushing the 'cock in the required direction. After that, it is up to the guns to hit their mark, and retrievers to gather the slain.

Some dogs display a clear distaste for snipe. Exactly the same aversion can be found when it comes to woodcock. Nobody has been able to determine what it is about these birds, which represent a gastronomic delight to humans, that some dogs turn their noses up at, but there is no getting away from the fact that they do. In some cases, this canine attitude may be virtually incurable. Most dogs can be brought around to snipe, but some never seem to get away from their prejudice to 'cock. The keen shooter will find himself holding his breath as his young dog is sent out on its first retrieve of a 'cock. Sometimes the bird will be picked without any trouble, in which case sighs of relief will be heard all round. In other cases, the 'cock will be picked with obvious distaste, but carried back. Even this is far, far better than the dog who either totally refuses to pick the bird or, alternatively, picks it up only to spit it out. In either of these latter cases of refusal, it is no bad thing to send out an older, more experienced dog in the hope that the youngsters will be overcome with jealously, snatch up the retrieve, and race back with it. The same situation can be contrived using a cold woodcock on the training field. Alternatively, if an experienced 'cock dog is not available to show the youngster the ropes, a good helping of patience, perseverance and cajoling; even throwing the bird a few yards with a string attached to it, and jerking it along the ground; should convince the hesitant pupil. Strangely, but thankfully, once this initial hesitancy has been overcome, most gundogs will take to woodcock, and snipe, like proverbial ducks to water.

As an alternative to springer spaniels and good working strains of cockers, another breed may be considered for driven 'cock shooting – the Irish water spaniel. This breed may have been given a bad press, and something of an 'incorrigible' reputation; being strong-willed and certainly not for the novice trainer but, in the right hands, they can be made up into excellent workers. Equally, while it is generally accepted that they are better recognised as retrievers with the accent on water work, rather than as 'true' spaniels; and despite the fact that their thick, curly coat is far from ideal for working in thick cover, the Irishman can show his worth as flushing 'cock, if suitably trained and controlled.

Glenstal Abbey in County Limerick was home to the Barrington family and widely recognised as among the best of Irish 'cock grounds in the years before 'The Troubles' after the First World War. The shoot was noted not only for the quality of its sport, but also for the high standard of its kennel of Irish water spaniels. These dogs were used to flush 'cock from the carefully managed coverts and then to retrieve the fallen at the end of each drive. A condition of invitations to shoot at Glenstal was that you should not bring a dog of your own. No doubt the pleasures of watching this famous kennel of dogs more than made up for having to leave a favourite Fido at home.

Many of the Irish 'cock shoots have now been broken up and, elsewhere, estates rarely feel that the employment of a full-time 'cock keeper can be seriously justified. All but a few sportsmen of the modern 'travelling syndicate' kind are looking for 'guaranteed sport' rather than the explanations and excuses associated with what is undeniably a not altogether reliable, migrant species. Keen and experienced 'cock and snipe shooters tend to be found, for that reason, among the ranks of farmers, the self-employed, and others who live nearby and can accept an invitation given with only a few days or hours notice. It was in this fashion that I enjoyed much of 'cock shooting in Argyll and Inverness-shire, and how I enjoy it today from the fringes of Galloway. It produces a class of sport in which the right sort of spaniel can be virtually worth its weight in extra woodcock at the end of the shooting day.

Four sportsmen makes an excellent party for this class of 'cock shooting, and the host will ensure that he picks the best men for the job. This does not necessarily mean that he will be looking for those who can shoot straight. That is a minor consideration compared to safety. There is seldom a place in the shooting field for a jealous, greedy gun, and least of all when shooting woodcock which have a habit of flying at head height, along and through the line.

Hosts and shoot organisers can make mistakes, however, perhaps in a misguided effort to entertain the bank manager, or other influential person. If you feel that your life is worth something more than an extra 'cock in the bag, but your neighbouring gun appears to be putting a lower value on it, you may presume to tell him of your differing opinion. If he persists,

Safety is of paramount importance on the 'cock shoot.

then you have three options open to you. Firstly, you can return his broadside. Secondly, you can grin and bear it. Thirdly, you can pack up and go home.

The first option can be very tempting but, with witnesses to the event, may get you into all sorts of trouble. The second possibility is a probability for those who do not receive many shooting invitations, do not want to upset anybody, and have neither the first hand knowledge or the imagination to picture the effects of a charge of shot at fairly close range. The third option is the one that I would take. After all, the dangerous shot can only continue to shoot in company because the company is prepared to stick it out.

Circumstances may allow a full frontal assault along the lines of striding up to the host and demanding, 'It's him or me. One of us is for home. Which is it to be?' However, in more normal circumstances, this would be whispered between drives. Or you might decide that, in order to save the host any embarrassment (certainly in those cases where the host is the perpetrator) it would be better to develop a quick case of 'Calcutta tummy', pains in the chest, a blinding headache, or whatever – just enough to mean you must stop shooting, but not so much as to necessitate a drive home from one of the party, or sending for an ambulance!

Leaving aside these darker aspects of shooting behaviour, let me assume that, as usual, the appointed hour has seen four keen, experienced and safe shooters gathering at the usual place. The usual pleasantries will be exchanged while battered Barbours and tweeds are donned. The sort of clothes that look as if they have arrived in the shooting field via the gardener and scare-crow, and all the better and more comfortable for it. On Scottish ground, very often, an attack on the sykes will have been planned.

A 'syke' is a small glen, associated with a burn rather than a river. Its sides may be clad in thick heather, scrub birch, bracken and assorted bushes. Where its sides ease out, it may produce quite wide, marshy areas where snipe and resting teal can be added to the bag.

Walking out a syke with four guns usually entails one man down at the floor and one man on either flank, directly in line. All three men will, for best results, be accompanied by a close-working spaniel. Alternatively, if the sykes on the ground over which you are shooting are quite wide, you may employ two beaters, stationed between the guns or, of course, two more guns to bring the numbers walking to five.

In either case, three or five, the remaining man is sent well ahead to stand and wait for any driven shots that may present themselves. And, in larger glens, this placing of extra guns may be extended to the point where there could be five guns in the walking line, a back gun trailing some 50yd behind them to take a shot at any 'cock that break back, a not infrequent occurrence, and two guns stationed ahead to take the driven birds. The possibilities and permutations are many, and can be altered easily to suit a specific set of circumstances.

A very similar system can be used for working the thick hedges that are a feature of some 'cock counties in the west of Ireland. One man is sent ahead, but keeps walking parallel to and slightly out from the hedge; a man without a dog and who will make a minimum of noise. He will be about 60yd or more in front of two men walking in line and working their spaniels into the hedge. A fourth man trails about 60yd behind, to take any 'cock that break back. Everybody must be certain of their safe angles of fire, and be of the sort who are not excited or flustered into taking a shot of which they are not 100 per cent certain does not risk their companions.

Where the party is smaller, and earlier in the season when the 'cock are still to be found lying on fairly open ground on the fringes of the moor, pointers and setters can come into their own. Indeed, some of the best bags in Islay, a Hebridean island far-famed for its 'cock shooting, were shot over setters by Edward

Laverack and others. Mild weather is what you need to get maximum results over setters. Harsh weather drives the woodcock down from the heather and light scrub into thicker cover where, as has been described, the close-ranging and staunch spaniel can prove itself the best companion for the 'cock shooter.

Out and about in September in pursuit of partridges.

CHAPTER FIVE

Rough Shooting

ROUGH SHOOTING IS ONE OF THOSE TERMS THAT GETS BANDIED about but is anyone sure of how it should be defined? Someone once wrote that it involves shooting over ground where a keeper is not employed. But that, surely, is only a half-truth because while the term obviously excludes driven shooting of coverts or moors, the fringes of formal shoots may provide some really outstanding 'rough shooting'.

Could it be defined as shooting which depends very heavily upon the quality of the dogs involved? Again, this might be seen to exclude driven shooting, but what about, say, walked-up grouse shooting where dogs are kept in at heel and only used for retrieving? It seems that the harder we try try to define 'rough shooting', the greater the confusion.

Rather than seeking an accurate definition, perhaps we should be considering the implications of the term. For one thing, it certainly suggests that there will be little formality to the sport, although this does not necessarily imply that driving is out, so long as it takes the form of impromptu 'mini-drives' with little if any reliance on unarmed beaters.

Equally, I do not see that the term 'rough shooting' should necessarily be considered to cover those rather specialist aspects of the sport that I have deliberately included in other chapters: snipe and woodcock, wildfowling, inland duck shooting, grouse walked up or shot over pointers and so on, although all and any of these might be included in a 'rough shooting' day. For the rough-shooter's bag should surely include a variety of game and other species.

Perhaps we can do no better than to admit that while rough shooting is hard to define accurately or by implication, we know what it is when we see it! When we read of Charles St. John working and shooting over his dogs with his gillie to help carry a bag of grouse, partridge, woodcock, pheasant, wild duck, snipe, teal, hares, rabbits, plover and the then unprotected jack-snipe and curlew, then we know without a doubt that he enjoyed a very fine day's rough shooting. It would still have been rough shooting if he had taken three or four companions with him. When we spend long, happy days hunting out hedgerows with our spaniels, walking through scrub woodlands and root crops, over marshes and then end up by waiting in ambush for flighting duck or roosting wood pigeons then we, too, have enjoyed a day's rough shooting.

Which breeds of dog prove the best companions for the rough-shooter? We are looking for dogs that can perform a general-purpose role. We want dogs that can both find and gather game. In my view, there are just two possibilities. These are either the spaniel, or one of the hunter-pointer-retriever breeds.

Those words may upset some people. They may choose to tell me about a retriever that will hunt, or a setter which will retrieve. I will not doubt their sincerity, because I have seen a number of such dogs in the field. But what I *will* say is that it is rare to see a Labrador that is capable of hunting as efficiently as a spaniel, or a setter that will retrieve as well as a good hunter-pointer-retriever and let me leave it at that.

How can a choice be made between a spaniel and one of the hunter-pointer-retriever breeds? Again, I am afraid that I am about to step on a few toes! It is enough to ask a dog to fulfil a dual role, let alone expect it to prove itself in the holy trinity. Therefore, being dogmatic, I would define spaniels as *hunter-*

retrievers and breeds such as the German-shorthaired-pointer, Vizla, Weimerarners and so on as *pointer-retrievers*.

I would certainly not risk a statement that implied that there were limitations to either of these types of usefulness, but I will stick my head out slightly by stating that the pointer-retrievers are seen at their very best on open ground such as the mixed terrain encountered where the grouse moor meets marginal land. Such a dog would have been an excellent companion for Charles St. John on his mixed bag days. Spaniels, on the other hand, seem totally in their element when faced with a more intimate shooting scene of thick cover, hedgerows and the like.

Equally, it has always seemed to me that when pointers are used, be they the specialists or the dual-purpose pointer-retrievers, the number of guns shooting over them should be limited. For example, if four men were gathered with four pointer-retrievers on the fringes of the moor, I would suggest that they might consider splitting into two parties. Pointers will work well as a brace but a quartet can lead to all sorts of strange noises erupting from their handlers. Spaniels, on the other hand, because of their relatively short-range quartering, covering a fairly narrow strip of ground in front of their master, are well suited to larger parties. Indeed, eight spaniels will work happily in front of eight guns and, if well trained and controlled, do so happily, productively, and without falling on top of one another.

There is another consideration which concerns the company in which you intend to shoot. If you are with keen spaniel men, they are not likely to appreciate your wide-ranging pointer crossing back and forth ahead of their spaniels. Indeed, pointers and spaniels are like oil and water; they do not mix, or at least they do not mix well.

As I have written about pointer work in other chapters, I will concentrate on spaniels for the remainder of this one and on those rough shooting occasions that involve a team of guns.

PARTRIDGE ORIGINS

Our fathers and grandfathers will talk of a time when you could expect a covey of partridges in virtually every field. They might be accused of looking back through rose-coloured glasses. Equally, there is no denying that the little brown bird has suffered a monstrous decline since those times when they were the bread-and-butter sport of British game shooting; both driven and rough.

In the days before the widespread use of inseciticides and adoption of silage instead of hay for winter fodder, when the combine was not so quickly followed by the plough, and countrymen still lived in a green and pleasant land, the rough-shooter's season would be underway, in a normal year, by the second or third week in September. For, despite it being legal to start partridge shooting at the start of the month, many birds are still immature cheepers at that time.

The normal practice, even on some of the best partridge manors would have been to make a start by walking-up the stubbles and roots. The alternative was to use pointers or setters. In fact, the fortunes of these two breeds have been closely linked to those of the partridge. Those who once saw a kennel of pointers as justifiable as, after a month on the grouse moors in Scotland, they could extend their seasons on their partridge grounds of England, tended to run down those kennels when partridge shooting declined, and in many places virtually disappeared.

The pattern of walked-up partridge shooting was firstly, to keep the birds within the boundaries of the shoot and, secondly, to concentrate them into the root crops which were still a widespread feature of mixed farming economy. In the early morning dew, the root crops would be wet and uninviting from the partridge's point of view, and so a start would be made on the stubbles or pastures, which would be walked-up so as to lead the partridge stocks into the root crops (such as turnips) with due regard to the weather, wind direction, and the lie of the land. No-one expected too much shooting during these opening moves. In the scant cover, the partridges would flush or run well ahead of the line. But slowly and surely the partridges were being persuaded into the roots which, in modern military terms, might be described as the 'killing ground'. It was here, in the dense cover, that birds would sit tight and allow the guns to get within range before they flushed.

The rules of root-walking were to pay close attention to keeping in line, and to safety angles when a shot presented itself; never to rush things and, at all times, to stay as quiet as possible. It was this form of shooting that prompted the old adage, 'game can see and game can hear', which, regrettably, some today seem to find so hard to remember. If they had served their time under some of the partridge-hands, they would soon have been made aware of the error of their ways if they had started to chatter.

Spaniels could provide sterling service in walking-up roots; a clever little partridge-expert ensuring that no birds were able to squat close while the line of guns passed them by, but never working so far out as to flush game beyond range.

A steady retriever, walking at heel, also had his opportunities to excel and many a Labrador gained a far-flung reputation on the basis of perhaps just a handful of exceptional retrieves. The gathering of game in roots, particularly when a shot bird carries on for some distance before falling, is beset with problems. Such work put great emphasis on the retriever's marking ability, or the handler's ability to direct the dog straight to the fall. An uncontrolled dog, seeking here and galloping there, would soon be flushing partridges all over the place. In some cases; when a runner was down and obviously strong; a handkerchief or stick might be left to mark its rough position and then, when the field had been walked out, the best dogs would be tried in turn. Could

A spaniel leaves no bramble unbashed, no thorn unthrashed, and no rabbit burrow uninspected in its search for game.

a mild wager, in such a situation, have been the origin of field trials?

LESSONS TO BE LEARNED

Partridge shooting may be little more than history in most counties, but I have described it because, besides being recognisable as the origin of rough shooting, its conduct in the past hold many lessons for the present.

Where game finding is carried out by those who are shooting, these men, beside their markmanship, must know what they are about. For example, if the old-time partridge shooters had simply walked through the root crops, because this was where the best of the shooting was to be enjoyed but had failed to start off by walking in the stubbles and pastures, their game-bags would seldom have been heavy. Rough shooting demands a close knowledge of the quarry's habits, and a generous helping of field-craft if it is to achieve the level of consistent success. It is all about being in the right place at the right time, and then knowing what to do when you are there. It is not, or should not be, simply a matter of a few friends marshalling themselves into a straight line, waving away their spaniels, and then proceeding over the shortest distance from one end of a field to the next. The best rough-shooters are highly skilled in the arts and crafts of their sport, and all their moves are carefully planned and considered.

The old partridge-shooters showed that in rough shooting, all gundog breeds can have their moments in the spotlight. Spaniels are great all-rounders on the rough shot but, certainly with just a couple of guns, can show their worth. And then, when a tricky runner is down in heavy cover such as a root crop, the previously superflous retriever, walking steadily at heel, can set about showing that extra 'polish' in gathering the fallen. It would be unfair to expect the jack-of-all-trades breeds to match the masters of the art of retrieving although, at times, individuals come very close to doing just that.

ROUGH SHOOTING PRACTICE

Variety is normally the spice of life on the modern rough shoot, even if one hundred pheasants are released and hopper-fed in order to supplement the wild stocks. This, surely, is one of the joys of rough shooting – you never really know what to expect. Varied terrain on the shoot, be it a patchwork of small fields, thick hedges and copses in the lowlands, or the fringes of the moor that take you past the lochan set on heather ground, through the birch scrubs, down sykes and glens and on to the marginal pastures, root crops and perhaps an oat stubble set close to the farm steading, make for the cream of rough shooting. And, whether you shoot over spaniels or pointer-retrievers, a common thread runs through the fabric of a day's sport.

The ground should be worked so as to turn birds into the shoot. On a rough shoot, by definition, the game is likely to be fairly thin on the ground. It pleases no-one to see a covey of grouse or partridges rising just outside shootable range and then tearing off over the boundary fence. So the normal practice is to start with the boundary fields or ground, walking in line but with the flanking gun on the boundary side sent well forward. The flanker either heads the bird back into the shoot or, if he cannot turn them, at least gets a chance to reduce their numbers as they depart.

The old partridge-shooters approach to root crops holds valuable lessons for present-day shooters faced with any area of heavy cover. If the guns forget themselves and start chattering to each other, or shouting at unruly dogs, any game that is in the cover may run rather than squat. They will not stop until they reach the end of the cover, and are faced with open space. Anyone who has walked a field of roots in unruly company will recognise the feeling that the field is apparently empty, until the guns are practically up to the fence. Then up pops a covey of partridges, bang go the guns and, while everyone is still fumbling to reload, whatever pheasants and partridges there may be are off in an almighty flush. This is not the way to fill the game-bag.

Partridge-shooters learnt that in heavy cover such as kale, with the guns spaced too far apart, birds would run back through the line, or squat and let the guns pass by. Without spaniels or pointers, the guns might have to close up to the point where they had barely 5yd between them. Obviously, with say, five guns, they could only cover a strip just 20yd wide. If faced with a 100yd wide field, they would have to take it out in strips, perhaps involving the guns wheeling at the end of each strip with a precision that the Brigade of Guards would admire.

The use of spaniels allows these strips to be extended. A properly trained and controlled spaniel will quarter 10yd in front of its master at most, and no more than 20yd to either side. Therefore, two men with spaniels can space themselves up to 40yd apart, knowing that their dogs will touch, nose to nose, before whipping round to quarter across and meet their neighbour on the other side, or the field boundary if they are on the flank. Thus, with five guns, all with spaniels, a strip of close to 200yd wide can be taken out at one go. Virtually the same width can be achieved by two men working pointers although, of course, they would have to give their dogs far more time in their extended quartering.

All this illustrates the need for dependable dogs. Take the case of the spaniels. If any of them fail to hunt to their full quartering allowance of 20yd on either side, gaps are created in the line and, unless the guns move closer to allow for this, birds will be passed without flushing. Equally, the spaniels must get on with their work quietly and efficiently, with minimum supervision. Any commands should be given by whistle, for this is far less disturbing to game than the sound of a human voice. It only takes two or three outbursts of, 'Come back here, you damned dog!' to ensure that game will scuttle ahead to flush in a bouquet only when dogs and guns are up to the field boundary.

Today pheasants might be regarded as the bread-and-butter species for the rough-shooter and, as already described, it may be decided to supplement them by rearing and release, albeit in very modest terms compared to a formal, driven shoot where a keeper is employed. In seeking out the pheasants, it is important to realise that, when flushed, they display a tendency to head back to the wood in which they roost although, of course, in the case of wild birds, this roosting place may not be known to the guns. Still, it is worth bearing in mind that if you spend the morning pushing pheasants back toward their home wood it will be worthwhile organising 'mini-drives' of these woods after the lunch break, half the party walking through the wood with their spaniels while the remainder cover the exit routes.

Most rough-shooters, however, when you talk of pheasants, will probably think about hedge-hunting. The standard practice is to send one or two guns ahead to act as 'stops' where, perhaps, the hedge is intersected by another field boundary. The rest of the party then hunt the hedge toward the stops. It takes a nice measure of tactical judgement to get this hunting party deployed correctly.

If there are four guns in the hunting party, two of them will act as beating guns, placing themselves on opposite sides of the hedge and just out from it. They will be working their spaniels in the hedge. This leaves two more guns. It may be wise to place one of these as a back-gun, trailing at least 50yd behind the beaters. Many a wily old cock pheasant has won his long spurs by breaking back low and not rising until he thinks he is out of range. Other pheasants will have been scuttling along the hedge, seen the stops, retraced their steps and, again, decided that the safest exit route is back down the hedge. If the back-gun is doing his job, a well-placed charge of No.6 shot will be ready and waiting.

In the real world, rather than a fictional ideal where all rough-shooters are accompanied by perfect spaniels who know the hedge-hunting game, the best spaniels will be involved in the beating. The stop's dog will only be required to retrieve, as will any dog accompanying the back-gun. The shoot organiser will think of these things, even if he does not actually mention them.

With one or two stops, the beater-guns, and one back-gun, one or two men may be left over. How they are positioned will depend very largely on the nature of the hedge, and the lie of the land. For example, if the hedge is thick and high, it may be that it *is so* thick and high that the back-gun will not see a bird fleeing down the opposite side, or not see it clearly enough to get a shot. In such cases, it may be wise to have two back-guns on opposite sides of the hedge.

Or it may be that there is a wood off to the side of the hedge, perhaps a field away. Remembering the pheasant's inclination to head for its roosting home when flushed, you might expect pheasants to swing out from the hedge and towards the wood. A flanking-gun, well back from the hedge and between the beater-guns and the stops, might enjoy a couple of high, sporting shots, particularly on sloping ground.

The possibilities and permutations are endless, and that, surely, is what rough shooting is all about.

It is the big driven day that attracts public attention but, for many shooters, the essence of their sport is to be out on the rough shoot, with just two or three friends and their dogs. And such days provide the time and opportunity to savour good dog work. A day's sport in Cumberland which I enjoyed last season provides an example of this.

By late morning, three men and four spaniels had bagged half-a-dozen pheasants from root crops and spinneys, and a couple of teal and a mallard which had sprung up from the farm ditches. An unusually unwary wood pigeon had also given itself up to us.

Northern rough-shooters may add grouse and blackcock to their bags.

104

We were walking along an old railway embankment when my companion's spaniel flushed a cock pheasant. It soared out and away from the embankment and, if we had placed a gun at the bottom, he would have had a high, testing shot. As it was, my companion shot it going away to his left.

The sound of his shot started another bird, a hen this time, which curved out and back, offering a wide, second shot. It somersaulted in a tight ball of feathers.

It was to this second bird that my companion's spaniel galloped, and with which it speedily returned. Then it was nonchalantly waved away to gather the cock that had fallen at the bottom of the embankment.

I should have said that the cock had positively crumpled and fallen all-of-a-heap. There seemed no doubt that it was dead. And so, as soon as my companion saw his spaniel racing back along the fence at the bottom of the embankment, he stopped it with his whistle, and then called it back to look again.

The dog spent a few seconds bustling about in the bracken and bushes where we thought the cock had fallen (our attention had really been on the second bird). But then he popped out and, once again, set off down the fence-back, nose to the ground and stern working furiously.

'Do you think he's rabbiting?' my companion called.

'Perhaps not,' I suggested. 'That bird looked stone dead, but your dog may know better.'

Two hundred yards down the fence, the spaniel proved himself. He suddenly turned at right-angles, raced into a tangle of gorse, then popped back out again with a very live pheasant held firmly in his jaws.

Any experienced rough-shooters who had seen good dogs working would not doubt it for a moment. It is such experience that gives you confidence in a dog. The confidence in him to leave him to get the job done, in however an improbable way it may seem. In just the same way, the experienced huntsman who knows his hounds will leave the best of them to make their own cast if they temporarily lose the scent of the fox.

Scent is a fascinating thing but unfortunately, in the sporting field, it is something that *we* can only speculate about, unless perhaps we are tracking an old, wild billy goat. But to a sporting dog, scent is what he steers by, and it is this power of scenting, and the experience which allows him to evaluate and decipher the signals his brain receives from his nose, that makes the brilliant dog stand apart from his less-gifted fellows.

In bringing this chapter to what may be seen as an early close, it might seem that I have not given rough shooting the space that it merits. However, the sport of rough shooting is a gathering together of many wide and varied aspects of the sport. This chapter has concentrated on the techniques of the old partridge-shooters and modern pheasant-chasers. I have looked at rough shooting in terms of walking-up fields and hedge-hunting but, of course, the sport extends far beyond these narrow confines. That is why this chapter is so short because, truth be told, virtually the entire book is about rough shooting. Most shoots can boast of at least an occasional woodcock, or some odd corners of undrained ground where snipe can be reasonably expected. These will be sought out by the rough-shooters in exactly the same ways described in the specialist chapter on woodcock and snipe. I have spoken in this chapter of the 'mini-drives' that can result from working pheasants back toward their roosting woods and this sport, albeit in a far less formal setting, is conducted along the same lines as any driven sport. The majority of rough shoots will also produce some duck for shooters, who know a good meal when they see it, to argue over when the bag is being divided. Few rough shoots ever have need of the game-dealer's van. Rough shooters enjoy the spice of variety in their diet as well as their sport; far more so than the syndicate man and his family who are more likely to feed on a staple diet of ten brace of pheasants each season!

Northern shooters may be able to add grouse and blackgame to their rough bags. Again, they are not mentioned because here they have a chapter of their own. So the list goes on with a pinch of this and a lashing of that to make up the delectable whole of rough shooting which epitomises the arts and crafts, knowledge and science, as well as the deepest pleasures and satisfactions of sport with the dog and the gun.

Hard going on the Invernesshire moor. The sportsman must be sensibly clothed.

CHAPTER SIX

Grouse

THE RED GROUSE HAS BEEN DESCRIBED AS THE 'KING' OF GAMEBIRDS. realm is found in the high, heather-clad hills. This king lays on fine entertainment over the rolling purple oceans, where honey bees drone and skylarks sing out their hearts to the heavens in praise of the glorious scene.

That all sounds a bit flowery, doesn't it? But grouse have that effect. There is something incredibly fine in being out on the heather hills, but attempts to put this feeling in words often can do no more than sound corny. Oh, the heather on the hills, and the roamin' in the gloamin' is best left to the designers of biscuit tins and tourist posters. So pay no attention to me while I slip out of my plus twos and into my kilt!

Grouse shooting, for many, particularly Americans, the Swiss and others from abroad, means driven shooting. Travel through the Derbyshire Peaks, on up through Yorkshire and Northumberland, across the Border into Peeblesshire, Dum-friesshire, Roxburghshire, Lanarkshire; drive north into Perthshire, Angus, Morayshire and Aberdeenshire, and you will see carefully tended moors. They are burnt into patchwork of young, short heather, and older, ranker stuff to provide a mix of food and shelter. Keep your eyes open for lines of butts. These come in all shapes and sizes. The ones that you are most likely to notice will be horseshoe-shaped structures of stone walling, with enough space inside for a sportsman with a pair of guns and a loader, a dog or two, and perhaps a spectator. When you see them, you know that you are in grouse driving country.

Beaters on the grouse moore bring in many miles of hill in one drive to the butts. They are spaced far apart, carrying their flags, but the grouse, particularly if they are caught out on short heather, will take flight at the merest sight of them, or not long after. Spaniels might be seen as useful helpers for the beaters when they are working the older, denser heather but, generally speaking, the driving of a moor is far more dependent upon man power than on good dogs.

However, dogs come into their own on the moor at the end of a drive. Many grouse, only a few of which may have been accurately marked by those doing the shooting, will have fallen in front of, and behind, the butts. With a perfect team of guns, most of the grouse will have fallen either some 40yd in front of the butts (first barrel kills) or almost on top of the butts (second barrel kills). But, in reality, even with the best regulated grouse-shooters, birds will be scattered here, there and everywhere. Nothing has changed since Sir Frederick Millbank advocated the use of spaniels to pick these birds as quickly and efficiently as possible. Spaniels, with their quartering patterns and noses close to the ground, will gather up these birds in superb fashion.

Further back, perhaps 200yd behind the line of butts, pickers-up will have been waiting and watching with the teams of high-performance gundogs. They will be looking for those birds that have not been killed cleanly and fly on for some distance before falling. On these marked, individual birds, as I have argued elsewhere, I do not think there is anything else to beat a Labrador or one of the less used, specialist retriever breeds. A good Labrador should be expected to be a master of the art of this type of retrieve; particularly when he has to 'get out into the country' to search for his bird.

It might be said that the driven grouse moor can be seen as one area of shooting where only the services of retrieving dogs, be they spaniels or the more specialist breeds, can be considered as absolutely indispensable. Just how vital their services are is shown by the fact that many experienced grouse moor owners, keepers and shooting men will tell you that good dogs will account for twenty per cent of the birds gathered, and as much as forty per cent of the total bag on some moors.

Another aspect of grouse shooting where dog work, other than for retrieving the fallen, can hardly be said to be at a premium is walking-up in the modern style. I say 'modern style' because it is a method perfectly suited to catering for the modern phenomenon of the travelling syndicate of eight guns.

The team is marshalled into a straight line, with approximately 40yd between each gun, although this space might well be occupied by a beater who will double up as a 'gun-bearer' carrying cartridges, shot birds and so on. Sometimes, when the moor is extensive, those who are new to the walked-up form of doing things may see the morning's sport as a route march from their dropping-off point, to a place where they rendezvous with a Land Rover carrying their light lunch and a reserve of cartridges, corn plasters and the like; followed by an afternoon's sport marching back whence they came. Such feelings will be heightened when the sun rides in a clear blue sky, and there is not a whiff of breeze to cool the melting brow. Despite all that, one thing is certain. Not very long after they have eased their aching feet in a tub of water, and their parched throats with a tumbler of whatever they fancy, they will be vowing to return. As I said at the start of this chapter, grouse and the scenery in which they are found have that effect on people.

Perhaps, thinks the keeper, next time they come north for a spot of hill walking and grouse shooting in August, they will leave behind their wellie boots, thick socks, heavy tweed breeks and caps, thick shirts, thornproof waxed jackets and anything else that a self-respecting Highland keeper would prefer he was not asked to carry when the party have barely got into their stride! Why is it that British sportsmen don green wellies and thornproofs, come rain, hail or shine?

WALKING-UP WEAR

What *should* you wear on the hill for a day's walking-up grouse, when the weather is hot and still, in late August or early September? We all have preferences, but here are a few words of advice from a grossly overweight, and heavy-smoking chaser.

Boots have to be leather. I wear leather boots even on a wet, boggy moor, because rubber boots, even those only of ankle length, overheat the feet. Perhaps they remind me of the methods used to build up stamina at my Naval school — endless circuits of the running track while wearing a diver's wet-suit under oilskins. The only good thing about that was finishing by sprinting down to the dock and leaping into the sea!

Boots should be well worn-in. Buy them in the spring, wear them for gardening and country strolls through the summer, and they should be ready for the hill in August. As an alternative to boots, some hill men wear shoes of the heavy, brogue type. Their ankles, however, must be equal to the strain, or immune to the sprain. Incidentally, if you soak your boots in neat's-foot oil (I use Carr's Leather Oil), they will be every bit as waterproof as rubber boots and, in my opinion, twice as comfortable. Commando-type soles are the standard choice, but do be careful when you are crossing wet rocks, particularly with a loaded gun in your hands.

Woollen socks are best, in hot or cold weather. If you find they are becoming too warm, then simply roll them down below your choice of light, but hard-wearing, breeches, kilt or shorts. In this department, the main object is to avoid anything tight or restrictive — which is where the kilt, worn in the fashion of the true Scot, is a winner all the way. However, as they say in the North, after a Scot invented the kilt, a fool of an Englishman invented barbed wire. Whether or not it is fair to blame the English, to negotiate a tight, wire fence in a kilt is certainly not easy. It is rather like having to land an aeroplane when you are not quite sure whether the undercarriage is down!

My alternative to the kilt in heat-wave weather is an ancient pair of khaki shorts in which a previous generation marched across North Africa and into Tunisia, button-flies, baggy-legs and all. But choose lightweight, cotton trousers if you know or suspect that the ground you will be covering has a tick problem.

How I hate ticks! You can try to burn them off with a cigarette, or wait till they have sucked their fill of your own or your dog's blood, and then roll them off. Or you can smother them in cooking oil or light machine oil and hope that it will clog their breathing pores and make them fall off immediately, or allow you to ease them off with tweezers half an hour later. As I discovered after one particularly strenuous day, up hill and down dale, the blood-sucking tick does not take too kindly to being smothered in 'Deep-Heat' or any similar, mentholatum rub. What you must *not* do is simply to try to pull them out. You will leave the head behind and increase the risk of infection. If you do simply attack them and, subsequently, a rash appears, accompanied by nausea or fever, you are well advised to waste no time in taking yourself off to the doctor who will explain to you that ticks can transmit certain diseases, including typhus! Incidentally, when you have disposed of your tick sensibly, wash the area with soap, and then give it a dab with some anti-histamine cream.

A light, cotton shirt is cool to wear, but you may notice the gun's recoil if you do not wear an outer layer, such as a waistcoat. Personally, I avoid the need for a waistcoat because I have all my guns fitted to me when I am wearing my thick winter tweeds. In summer, I use a slip-on recoil pad which brings the gun's stock to the required extra length, as well as reducing recoil.

Do not wear a tie. The only time when it is worth putting something around your neck is in really hot weather, when you should use a large, cotton handkerchief that has just been dipped in a cool, mountain stream. Much the same can be said of hats and caps which, if worn at all, by those who are a 'bit thin on top', should be of the very lightest weight material. Some Americans can be seen sporting rather 'Ramboesque' versions of their popular peak cap in camouflaged material which are 'topless', like a tennis player's sun-visor. Normally, however, unless you are shooting very early or late in the day, the sun is so high in the sky that it does not present a problem.

Walking-up in a party is a fine, shooting experience, and it can give your dog some interesting retrieves from time to time. You may also work a close-hunting spaniel in front, although (dare I suggest) this may be more for your own or your dog's amusement. Unless the heather is particularly rank and high, the problems of walked-up grouse shooting are far more likely to be concerned with getting within range of the grouse before they take to the wing, rather than flushing them from close to your feet. Steeply-rolling ground is a great advantage on many walked-up grouse moors as it allows the guns to appear suddenly on the brow of a hill, virtually on top of any grouse that might happen to be squatting on the opposite side.

I have to admit, however, that this is something of an introduction to what I find unsatisfactory about walking-up in line. It does not allow much freedom of choice to the individual, or allow him to use his game-sense and field-craft. To me, it seems to impose the formalities of the driven shoot onto what should, at its best, be an informal scene. Of course, this is no more than an admission of personal preference.

Alternatively when walking up alone, or in a small party, it is possible to adopt more of the 'rough shooting' approach. You must know what you are about, have a close knowledge of the quarry's habits, and good field-craft to be able to get on terms with grouse. Good dogs can be material aids to your sport. You may choose to walk-up with no more help than that offered by a steady retriever, as advocated by Lord Walsingham for those hard days when his nose bled and the hardest of keepers shed their jackets. This is a method best suited to quite heavily-stocked ground. It is where the stock of grouse is thinner on the ground, the terrain is broken, and the heather is high and rank, that spaniels and pointers will prove their true worth.

CHOOSING TYPES OF DOG

Any suggestion made as to which type of dog is most likely to fill the bag is likely to lead to all sorts of curses being thrown in my direction. The only thing more dangerous and daunting will be, later in this chapter, to make some humble observations on the development of the specialist pointer and setter breeds. Now there *is* a minefield that I might do better to walk around, rather than through!

But returning to the question of spaniels versus pointers on the moor, instead of making my normally rash statements, I shall just introduce the subject with a short story.

One man was devoted to his spaniels. Another was very keen on his pointers. I heard the story, from their own lips, of the time when they found themselves shooting over neighbouring moors of thinly-stocked ground in the West Highlands. Each claim that it was the other who was extolling the merits of his own dogs and that in order to put him in his place, a small competition and wager was suggested. Each man would take a brace of dogs, and shoot over their own. The loser would pay for that night's dinner and drinks. As it turned out, they shared the cost of the evening's entertainment, because both men shot five brace!

What amused me most, however, was when, many years later, the spaniel man was defending his choice of breed to me on the grounds that he could shoot fewer grouse over them than any man with a pointer. Conservation to the fore, as and when it suits, I thought to myself!

The point that he was trying to make was that an energetic

115

gun with a team of good pointers might easily overshoot a moor if, instead of thinking of the population's long-term good, he set about harrying them into extinction. A covey is found, flushed, and two of their number downed. An eye is kept on the rest and, having either seen them pitch down, or having surmised where they are headed, a man or men and dogs make a beeline for them. Unfortunately, this sort of thing can happen both on commercialised shoots and those estates where, dare I say it, a new owner may know rather more about making money than he does about game management and sporting ethics. But, make no mistake, it can happen just as easily with either pointers *or* spaniels.

More caring sportsmen would far rather head off in a direction that will not take them to the survivors of the covey, at least not time, after time, after time. These are the same sportsmen who will take a quiet pride in concentrating on old, barren birds, or the parent birds that spring first and lead the covey. The sort who will be distressed to see immature grouse from late broods being deliberately shot at the start of the season, to the point where they would rather pack up and go home than continue shooting.

On the question of spaniels versus pointers, I really do wonder whether it is wise to say anything more than that it is probably best left to the individual to choose. Some of us manage to enjoy both alternatives. Others become quite partisan in extolling a particular point of view. Spaniels will appeal to those visitors to the moor who already have spaniels and who do not like to hang about too much. Shooting over spaniels tends to involve walking rather longer distances, but covering a narrower strip of ground. Pointers, on the other hand, being far wider-ranging, do tend, in general terms, to lead to a rather less strenuous forward movement, covering a shorter distance, but a much wider strip of ground. Either long and narrow strip or shorter but wider strips. At the end of the day, in terms of the actual area of ground covered, there may not be all that much in it.

One aspect of pointer work which does, however, turn whatever logic there might be in this discussion based purely upon ground coverage, is the pratice of running pointers in a brace, with a second brace held in reserve. When the first brace of pointers show signs of tiring, they are called in and leashed, while the second are loosed. Then, while this second brace are running, the first brace are resting in readiness to replace the second when they tire.

This may mean, of course, that the guns shooting over the pointers have to be attended not only by a dog handler, but also a second assistant to take the brace that are resting. In such circumstances, it would not be fair to make comparisons with spaniels unless they, also, were run and rested in this fashion.

When I write about 'pointers' I am, of course, including setters be they Gordon, Irish or English. These three setter breeds, and pointers, all run against each other in trials.

I think, it is not such an insignificant factor that, in these trials, the dogs run, often for a relatively short time, then have a long rest before running again. Nor, perhaps, is it insignificant that many of those handling the dogs are dog people, first and foremost, and shooting people second, if at all. It has crossed my mind, from time to time, to wonder how much this has affected the *type* of dogs in the pointer, setter category. 'Horses for courses' and, if you want a sprinter, then that is the type for which and from which, you breed.

How differently the pointer and setter breeds might have evolved if more of those shooting over them were also handling them; in other words those who were primarily interested in shooting, and saw their dogs more as a means to an end, rather than an end in themselves. And, if they wanted to shoot over the same individual or brace of dogs throughout a long day on the moor, without the encumbrance of reserve dogs, would breeding

Pointers are normally run in relays of two working and two resting.

policies have paid a little bit more attention to stamina, and a little less to speed? I remember that quite recently, at a pointer and setter trial, I heard a conversation along the following lines which did make me wonder.

'My goodness. How well the Gordons have been coming on in recent seasons,' one lady handler said to another.

'Yes,' replied her companion. 'Twenty years ago they were all such plodders, setting their own pace as if they expected to be running all day.'

Well, all I can say is that such comments might well be considered by those seeking reasons why despite, as outlined many times in this book, there are still many shooting situations which seem to cry out for the services of a pointer or setter breed, these breeds have gone, in the course of the last century from being among the most among the least favoured breeds of gundog with shooting owners! As I say, just a thought that might bear some consideration, particularly in view of the soaring interest in the imported pointer-retriever breeds over the last half-century.

Having got that off my chest, it may seem a total about-face to say that grouse shooting over modern pointers and setters is one of the finest sports I enjoy. Ironically, it has very little to do with the shooting, as I discovered at field trials held before the opening of the shooting season. On such occasions, everything is done in the normal way, up to the point where the grouse are flushed. Then a shot of salute is fired straight up into the air, rather than at the departing birds, to test the dog's reaction. Watching these dogs is enough; just to see the products of a small band of devoted breeders and trainer-handlers whose interest in bloodliness, genetics and animal psychology might put the Jockey Club to shame.

A DOG'S DAY

They say that every dog has his day and perhaps this is never so true as when we are looking at the pointers and setters. Their handlers will talk of the conditions that suit an individual dog, rather like racehorse trainers who know which of their charges prefer soft or firm ground. A graphic example of this is given by Dugald Macintyre in his book *Wild Life of the Highlands*, relating his experiences between the two world wars.

At the time when he was keepering in Kintyre, he had some excellent pointers. He relates how a party of field trial judges, on a busman's holiday, had a fortnight's shooting over his team of five dog pointers. At the end of the fortnight, the judges declared that Macintyre's was the best team they had ever seen or shot over, but they could not agree on which was the best individual, so they asked Macintyre which he thought was best:

> *I was really not quite sure myself, so I said, 'Old Dee is best in a breeze because he keeps his head so high; Old Spey beats him at roading, and Islay at ranging.' I knew perfectly which dog a field trial judge would consider best at a short trial; that was Little Sam, who could make rings round the other members of the team for speed of ranging and spectacular pointing. But I named Old Spey as the best dog. If birds were wild, it was Spey alone who had the secret of making them sit, and if they would not sit to him, it was no good trying another dog.*

Dugald Macintyre went on to describe Old Spey's *modus operandii*. He took a very workmanlike approach, going over his ground quietly and with the ability to pick up the very merest hint of scent at outstanding ranges. Sometimes, a gun would be forced to ask whether or not the dog was actually pointing because, at the start, he might be standing in a fairly relaxed attitude, with only his twitching nostrils giving the hint that he had winded something. Then he would suddenly set off on a rush of about 100yd, at the end of which Old Spey would come to a 'real' point. But he was only waiting for his handler and the guns to catch up, and then away he would go again. The next point would be of greater intensity, and everyone then realised that Old Spey had led them right up to a covey, for which they were ready and waiting when he was sent forward to flush them out.

Another example of Spey's abilities was shown on an occasion when, having taken the shooting party to one covey, from which five birds were shot, and Spey having dropped to the sound of gunfire, he raised himself straight into another pointing attitude. He led the guns on through the fallen grouse to another brood 100yd further on.

Incidentally, those who spend their time being dragged across moors by pointers being held in reserve on leads will be interested to know that Spey walked happily to heel while other pointers worked, and would even 'back' them from that position.

Dugald Macintyre went to extol Old Spey's many virtues but, rather than my listing them, let me reiterate Macintyre's conviction that Little Sam of speed and style would be thought, by the judges at a short field trial, to have run rings round the dog which, in Macintyre's opinion, was far and away the better shooting dog. And so Little Sam would have stacked up the wins and prizes, gained the titles, and have been sought out, and commanded the highest fees as a stud dog, whereas Old Spey might have been an 'also ran' and even written-off as 'a bit of a plodder', despite his game finding ability.

Old Spey's ability to make grouse sit to him, to the extent that if they would not it was no good trying another dog, would have become more and more useful as the season progressed. Grouse that have been shot at over pointers are, by the middle of September, getting to know the name of the game. They are flighty, and will not sit well to dogs or man. Soon, on driven moors, the coveys will be joining into packs, seeking safety in numbers as they cross the line of butts. It is now, on the dogging moor, that a little bit more thought and planning may be required. Some find that the solution to 'flighty' birds is to walk them up but with the intention not so much of getting a shot as to moving them into areas of thicker heather which provides good holding cover. It is now, with the grouse exactly where they are wanted, that the more experienced and less exuberant pointers in the team can lead their guns into range before the birds spring.

Grouse shooting over pointers is traditionally conducted in pairs. Each party of two guns would expect to have two gillies; one to take the reserve brace of dogs, and another to carry the game, spare cartridges and so on. Alternatively, a spare brace of dogs would be brought up with the pannier pony that carried the lunch, and then the grouse. The only individual, on such occasions, was the keeper of whoever was handling the working dogs. If there were four guns, this would require a duplicate term of attendants and dogs. Admittedly, this is a rather formalised picture but it does, I hope, serve to give some idea of how the sport was conducted and, most significantly, that only two guns would be involved at each point. Today, on some moors, this has changed. The most extreme case of which I have heard involved six Italian paying guests, each with a three-shot repeater, all insisting on shooting at each and every point. Besides any other considerations, this sort of thing can hardly be considered as 'sporting'. Even with fairly indifferent marksmanship, with eighteen shots ripping into them, a covey is likely to be annihilated. Surely, the proper culmination of a pointer or setter's work is, at most, four clearly separated and selective shots, rather than something reminiscent of machine-guns opening fire on the first day of the Battle of the Somme.

This is not to say that there is anything wrong with a larger party of guns following a brace of pointers, but the guns should draw lots and take their turn. This is not such a loss except for the man without a soul, who will not recognise the finer points of a dog's work, and to whom shooting over pointers must seem a rather sorry spectacle. In its own way, shooting over pointers is similar to stalking deer in that the actual shot is something of an anti-climax, but a necessary culmination to the sport already enjoyed by man and dog.

HUNTER-POINTER-RETRIEVERS

Before closing this chapter on grouse shooting, I should perhaps say something about the role of the HPR (hunter-pointer-retriever) breeds. After all, we are seeing more and more of them on the moors as they become widely accepted throughout the land as fulfilling a general-purpose role. The man who shoots grouse for only a week or less in the season would find it hard to justify a specialist breed such as a pointer or setter but an all rounder, that can prove itself equally useful on the driven shoot, out wildfowling, or hunting hedgerows, might be viewed as 'just the thing'.

The harsh truth of the matter is, however, that anyone who decides upon an HPR must accept it for what it is. A jack-of-all-trades, but master of none. Anyone who expects their HPR to hunt as well as a spaniel, point as well as a pointer, and retrieve with the polish of a Labrador will, I am afraid, be setting himself up for disappointments.

This is reflected in the manner that HPRs are judged at a field trial. For example, they are allotted marks for steadiness with the possibility that, while they may be slightly defective in this respect, they can make up the points in other aspects of their work. Spaniels, retrievers, pointers and setters simply cannot get away with that sort of thing.

An acquaintance told me of what he had seen at one HPR trial where the best of the bunch, working over a good dogging moor, was a Brittany. Even she flushed a number of single birds before making a positive point. And then she moved in and flushed without orders, and not allowing time for the two guns to come up into position. She was then eliminated for having broken her point but note that if she had held it, she would not have been eliminated for bumping the earlier, single birds.

The truth of the matter, surely, from the shooting man's point of view was that this Brittany would not have provided even one shot to the guns. And she was described as the best of the bunch.

But there is, of course, another side to the coin, as anyone who has seen and enjoyed productive work from HPR breeds on the moor will testify. Taken on its own, this story of bumping birds and broken points could be seen as a condemnation of all HPRs, but I am wondering whether, in truth, the dogs involved in this trial were simply lacking in grouse experience. I have heard it said that many owner-handlers of HPRs seem unaware that there is the world of a difference between lowland and moorland. The HPR who has done well on pheasants and rabbits may simply not realise what is expected on open, heather moorland, where they may not really know the scent that they are looking for. If that is so, and the HPR *afficionados* want their dogs to be taken more seriously on the moors, then they should give their dogs plenty of moorland experience before entering them in moorland trials.

There is also the question of range and stamina. Pointers, in particular, are thoroughbred, ground-covering machines with a beautifully smooth running action. They flow over a moor in a fashion against which the majority of HPRs look positively clumsy, and which puts far greater strains on the HPR's stamina.

No doubt the HPR breeds would improve if given more work on grouse, and by being bred selectively with a view to improving their running action. But then we enter a 'Catch-22' situation as the man who could give them such experience, and look toward establishing a better gallop, is more than likely to be deeply committed to the pointer, or one of the setter breeds already!

A wildfowler's dog may have to work in thick, clinging mud as well as harsh weather conditions.

126

CHAPTER SEVEN

Duck and Geese

DUCK AND GEESE ARE PERHAPS THE WILDEST OF WILD QUARRY SPECIES
to be found in Britain. They are ever alert to danger and, in the
wide, open spaces that they often inhabit, can see it coming long
before it gets within shotgun range. That is why there is little if
any need for dogs to hunt, flush or point where wildfowl, or
waterfowl as they are known in America, are concerned. What
the wildfowler needs is a good retrieving dog, and nothing more.
A dog which, as we shall see, must be hardy, strong and full of
the character that might be described as 'true grit'. But first we
must know something of the quarry and its habits.

MORNING AND EVENING FLIGHTS

Duck have become nocturnal feeders. Why this should be so is
open to question. But they will spend the daylight hours in
resting or preening on the sea or a large area of water or some
secluded spot that affords them shelter from predators. At dusk,
the duck will fly out from these 'sanctuaries' and spread
themselves over a large area in their search for food. In the early
part of the season, duck-shooters will watch the stubble fields for
signs of their quarry. Then their attention turns to freshwater
marshes, saltings and flight ponds. Flight ponds, which may be
little more than an area about half the size of a tennis court,
created by a fairly impromptu damming of a stream, or a much
more elaborate affair, can be 'fed' with barley and frosted

127

potatoes to maintain the duck's interest through the season, provided that they are not shot too regularly.

Knowing this, we see two main opportunities for shooting duck, both of which involve something of an ambush. We can either wait for them at dusk, as they arrive on their feeding grounds, or in the early morning, when they return to their resting places. We normally shoot duck on their arrival, rather than on their departure. Looking at the dusk flight, for example, it should be obvious that however many ducks may be sitting on a loch and feeling hungry, once a shot is fired they will be up and away in the briefest time. Their entire population will have been made aware of this assault upon their privacy and will be reluctant to return, certainly for days, and possibly for weeks, if they find an alternative, quieter spot. At the arrival point, however, the duck will be coming in dribs and drabs. The light will be fading fast when the first duck comes in. The flight may start with a trio of mallard, then a small group of teal, followed by a singleton, then a pair. Duck may be coming in long after it is too dark to see them, and it is these duck that will return on the following night, drawing in others, and ensuring that it will not be too long before you can shoot a pond for the second time. As long as some birds are allowed to come in in peace, you can shoot a flight pond perhaps once a fortnight, right through the season.

As far as dog handling is concerned, the dusk flight can be a fairly frustrating time. If you have been foolish enough to believe some writers, you may have been prepared to take an unsteady dog with you; a dog that will 'run in' when a duck falls or, even worse, whenever a shot is fired. At least if there *is* a duck to be retrieved, the dog should soon be back with you. If not, the dog might be splashing about for the next twenty minutes, searching for something that simply is not there to retrieve. Duck are not so foolish as to drop into a pond when a dog is tearing about and, anyway, the dog will steal your attention when you should be concentrating to hear the 'wicker of wings' that will turn your eyes in the direction of duck shadowing across the dimly lit sky.

Far, far better, I think, unless the retrieve is particularly straightforward, to keep the dogs with you in your place of concealment, until you think that you have had enough shooting. Remember to leave plenty of time for enough 'tail-enders' to come in and ensure that the flight will be continued. And then let the dogs go.

If the dog emerges out of the rushy gloom with a duck in his mouth which he places into your hand, you will be well pleased if this is his first flight. But if he then refuses to go out again, not seeming to understand what is required of him, and you know that there are four duck still to be picked off the pond and from among the reeds, you may not be so pleased. It may be your own fault. You may not have given your dog the right sort of 'dry' experience.

In the chapter *Thoughts on Training*, I have outlined some ideas on how a retriever might best be trained on the basis that, as often as not, there may be three or four birds to be picked, rather than a singleton. Rather than one dummy, the trainer may require half-a-dozen to be thrown into cover, out of sight of the dog. A step on from this is to train your dog in the dark. The procedure is simple. For the first few occasions, use a field of close-cropped grass; it could be a park or large lawn. Take your dog to this field after dark. Throw out three dummies, let the dog wait for a few minutes, and then send him out to retrieve, then again, and again. In a few weeks time, perhaps in early August before a young dog's first season he should be taken to the shores of a loch or pond, just after dark, when finishing touches can be added with perhaps two or three dummies thrown onto open water, and a couple more thrown in or close to a reed bed. In this way when the shooting season starts, the dog will have a grounding in what is required on its first visit, in earnest, to a flight pond.

You may find at the end of such a training session that you

only have four dummies, instead of five. Do not worry unduly. Similarly on the flight pond, if there is anything left to gather, you can always return in the morning. Unless of course, where ducks rather than dummies are concerned, you are beaten by a prowling fox!

There can be a frustrating aspect to the evening duck flight, particularly in those areas where shooting pressure is high. The duck may wait until it is late and then, all too soon, the night is completely black. But the brevity of the sport is surely part of its charm. And it has its exceptions, for example, when moon, time, tide and rough weather coincide to produce perfect conditions to flight wigeon at night on the saltmarsh. This, surely, is the very essense of duck shooting, and what better friend and companion to share it with than a tried and trusted dog?

The morning flight is a rather different affair. Now, instead of the ducks spreading out, they are concentrating back into their resting places. If their resting place is far out at sea, there is very little that can be done unless the tide is high and the weather rough, which may force the duck to seek shelter on the saltmarshes where, with cunning and field-craft, you may enjoy some good sport.

If, on the other hand, they are returning to a lake or loch, your chances are far more certain. The plan is be settling into hides on the shores of the loch, or possibly even being transported out to islands by boat, well before the first glimmering of dawn. Rough, squally weather is far and away the best, so dress accordingly in a warm tweed coat, cap, a woollen scarf and shooting gloves. How cold is that hour before the dawn! Rough conditions should delay the arrival of the returning duck, ensure that they will not be flying too high over the shoreline, and mask the sound of shooting to other duck that are still some little way off.

I stated that duck will not be flying too high in squally conditions, and, in retrospect, this may create the wrong impression. Rough weather *should* ensure that at least some of the duck will pass within range. Those who have believed that a driven pheasant is the most difficult shot, cannot, in my opinion, have shot many duck in squally conditions. Wigeon may figure in the bag, now that so many of them have adapted to inland habitats and habit. Here come a pair, fast and high, leaving you wondering just how much lead you should have given them. Four teal coming straight at you, intent on making a landing. You check your safety-angles, for you are not alone. They come whiffling in, spilling wind from their pinions. In the same second that you start to raise your gun, they explode into turbo-charged, vertical flight, whipping up, back and away with the wind and leaving you swearing that they performed backwards somersaults. Three mallard sneak in from behind, but you manage to drop the tail-end drake at extreme range. That will be a good swim for your dog. So it goes on. In the right place at the right time and given the right combination of conditions, you may bless the gloves that were saving your fingers from the cold only a few minutes ago, but are now saving them from the heat of the gun barrels.

There are estates where the duck's peace is carefully maintained on all but one or two mornings of the season, when things are judged 'just right' by the host and his keeper. Invitations are issued at short notice, and men may gather with their loaders, carrying pairs of guns.

Such shooting does not fall within the scope and spirit of the true wildfowler but, besides the shooting skills involved, shoots of this type offer a supreme challenge to dogs. The normal practice is to leave the pick-up until the host has signalled for shooting to stop, with late arrivals still turning overhead. Ducks that have fallen dead on the open water are the most obvious ones to start with. These can, however, create plenty of problems. In a choppy wave, with the swimming dog's eyes only a few inches above the water, his field of vision is strictly limited, and a dog that will

131

work to hand signals can save a great deal of your time and his energy. It should also be able to steer such a dog away from a winged duck which will dive, dive and dive again whenever the dog approaches, to the point where the exhausted dog may give up in disgust. Leave such a duck in peace, and it will naturally head ashore or at least into shallower and more confined water where a dog who has learned to dive after his duck will stand a better chance of catching it. Such retrieves are long remembered.

Then the shoreline must be worked for dead ducks and cripples. If there is thick mud, this can be the very devil of a job. The strength of even the strongest dog is quickly sapped in 'ploutering' through mud after a duck that keeps just ahead of him. An obedient dog can be called off until the crippled bird is given a charge of small shot; a 'cripple-stopper' as the punt-gunners would say.

WILD FLIGHTS

The true wildfowler concerns himself with wild flights on the salt marshes, below the high tide mark. In normal weather, the morning flight will be a poor affair, if any sort of an affair at all. Anyone who has been on the shore in the hour before dawn, will testify that while duck returning to their salty roosts are often heard, they are seldom seen. No; you must have really hard weather, and plenty of it, for a good wild flight. The numbers of duck on the coast will be swelled by those frozen off inland waters, and small parties of duck will be seen flying restlessly throughout the day. Heavy snow may create a regular flight. An onshore gale behind a rising tide can do the same. But it will not be too many days before shooting stops. Wildfowlers have always known that duck are concentrated toward the coast in hard weather. If the hard weather is prolonged, the birds become thin and unwary from hunger and exhaustion. No-one should want to shoot fowl that have reached this stage. Lest anyone be tempted, there are legally enforced, hard weather bans.

Incidentally, one might wish that these hard weather bans were extended to 'twitchers' – those so-called bird watchers who seem to know little and care even less. I have heard from one warden at a nature reserve that car and bus loads of brightly clad 'townies' were constantly harrying the duck, by approaching ever closer with their binoculars and note books to the point where duck in large numbers, having been driven back and forth across the countryside, succumbed to exhaustion in their weakened state and died. It does seem that many of those who have jumped on the green bandwagon out of fashion, rather that commitment, travel on an intellectual plane where ignorance is bliss.

GEESE

Geese, unlike most duck, follow the habit of resting at night and feeding during the day. Living on the Solway Firth gives me the privileged company of its world-famed wintering populations of greylags, pinkfooted and protected barnacles. Other geese winter here, but these are the 'big three'.

The pinks and grey spend their nights on sandbanks out from the shores of Priestside, Caerlaverock and Mersehead. In the first glimmer of dawn, singletons and pairs may flight over the shoreline, where eager wildfowlers crouch down in the mud and grass in an effort to conceal themselves. Then, suddenly, the air is filled with the sound of geese. A wildfowler raises his eyes for a quick glimpse at the goose armies rising from the sands, a mile or more away. The sky fills with regiments and brigades of geese flying in skein formation. A muttered curse will be heard at Priestside when it is realised the geese are headed toward the Brow Well. Position will, however, be irrelevant on those nine mornings out of ten when the weather allows the geese to gain height until, as their wavering lines come over the shore, there are four or five gun-shots high. Of course, that will not stop some

Perhaps dreaming of some warmer place.

'cowboy' from trying his luck.

True wildfowlers, on such mornings, just shrug their shoulders at the high fliers. It is enough just to have been there; to have breathed the tang of salt air and to have seen the dawn of a new day.

The alternative, tame way of doing things is to prepare an ambush on the goose feeding grounds. Decoys may be used to fool the approaching skeins into believing that all is well. Here come the leaders, whiffling down as they spill air from their wings, to be met by a fusillade of shots from the party of lads staying at the local hotel. This can be acceptable, if done in moderation, and under the supervision of a sensible and caring professional guide. But, on more than a few occasions, I have seen or heard of bags of geese shot on their feeding grounds which, quite frankly, have left me with a feeling of disgust.

Then there is the evening flight as geese return from their feeding grounds to their resting place. They tend to follow their usual practice of crossing the shore at heights way above shotgun range. But given an onshore gale, perhaps with snow or sleet, and the knowledge of where to intercept them, a boy with his first gun, as I remember so well, will be in with the chance of bagging his first goose.

THE WILDFOWLER'S DOG

I have done no more than skim over the great sport of wildfowling. The pursuit of duck and geese can become an all absorbing passion. But my aim, in a book centred on sport with the dog and the gun, is to highlight some of the features of the sport that we must consider in our choice, training and care of a wildfowling companion.

Inland flighting, be it of duck on fed ponds or geese on their feeding grounds, might not seem to put any great demands on a dog, except that it should be a clever retriever. The duck dog, as we have seen, has to be literally up to the task of 'working in the dark' but the inland, morning goose-shooter needs little more than the services of a covert-trained dog, albeit one which might, on occasion, be expected to get really far out into the country in pursuit of a winged goose.

No, it is not so much the 'tame' situations that I am thinking about but both the strains that might be put on a dog after large-scale, morning duck flights, and even more significantly, the rigours of wild flights on the shore.

Look at virtually any book concerned with wildfowling and you will find advice on what clothes to wear on the shore. Below the waist, don two pairs of heavy socks, long johns, pyjama trousers, track suit bottoms under a pair of loose fitting, warm trousers over which you have waders and short, waterproof overtrousers. Above the waist, a vest, warm shirt, one thin and one thick pullover, a quilted waistcoat, woollen scarf or towelling cravat, shooting mitts and so on, all under a waxed jacket. Great space may then be given to a discussion of the merits of various items of headgear ranging from deerstalker's with ear flaps to woolly balaclavas. I have seen a model wearing a new 'polar' suit, imported from America – he was also wearing a big smile in the obviously bitter conditions. But the wet, shivering spaniel, sitting at his heel was not smiling.

If you have not done so already, please stop to think about your fowling dog. He may, like you, have become used to living in a centrally-heated environment. How would *you* like to be dragged down to the foreshore on a gale-torn morning, when snow or sleet are taking your breath away, wearing nothing more than your normal shirt and trousers. Sitting there in three inches of water and oozing mud, it sounds worse than cruel. Yet it is nothing more than many fowlers put their dogs through, without a second thought. Sometimes, the dog will be an old grey-beard, feeling the first creaks of rheumatism in his joints.

It might be better if we could do without the services of a dog for wildfowling. It is one thing to commit ourselves to long hours in harsh conditions, but what about our faithful friend who has just gathered a duck from water whose temperature is just above freezing, and who now has to sit in an icy wind?

Part of the solution to the dilemma of needing a dog for fowling is to choose a puppy from a tough breed, and keep it that way. This means one of the specialist water dogs. The curly-coat has long ago died out of fashion, but their coat turned any amount of water, and they were courageous and hard. Irish water spaniels are in their element in mud and water and are keen and active; perhaps just a little bit too much so for some of us and, again, they are rarely seen. Chesapeake Bay retrievers certainly have the right credentials and origin but, personally, I have not seen what these imports to our shores are capable of doing. That leaves us with the Labrador and, without a doubt, this is far and away the favourite choice as a fowler's companion.

However, in choosing a Labrador, be aware that there are definable 'types' in the breed. For example, the trialler, and certainly those who seem almost to view working tests as an end in themselves, may go for very fast, stylish dogs. Many shooting men, on the other hand, particularly those whose shooting is of the driven kind, seem to incline toward a dog that has equal dimensions in height, length and sometimes width.

This distinction is even more clearly seen when comparing the average 'working' Labrador to its modern show-style counterpart. Those seeking to produce the 'perfect worker' in terms of a dog for trials, tests and picking-up seem to have ignored the traditional appearance of the breed. In fact, they have produced what some might describe as black or yellow whippets. Some would say that it does not matter what a Labrador looks like, so long as it works with pace and style. And so they do not mind if the dogs they are breeding are tall and lean with narrow heads and snipey noses, with cat-like paws and a ratty tail, just so long as they go like stink. But how pathetic such thin-coated dogs look when they are asked to wait shaking and shivering by their owner's peg on a wet shooting day, or in icy conditions on the foreshore.

Ironically, it is maybe the modern show dog that is best suited to be out and about when the going gets tough. This is due to the Kennel Club's insistence, in its breed standards, that a successful show dog must exhibit those characteristics considered to have a direct bearing on its abilities as a working retriever and, in particular, one that should cope happily with being in water as much as it is out. A show judge looks for a weatherproof, double coat, a powerful, otterlike tail, and a strong head and neck.

Many working strains of Labrador have lost the fine head and kind expression that were once so clearly associated with the breed. Their coats are too thin, their tail is too thin to aid them in swimming, and they just do not have the power of the old-time dog.

There are, of course, exceptions to the rule. There are still some working strains that carry all the right hallmarks of a Labrador bred for intelligence as well as speed, and gritty stamina as well as style. Just look at a photograph of the dogs keeping company with the Duke of Wellington, or the late Sir Joseph Nickerson to see what I mean.

The true, *fowler's* Labrador is a hardy, courageous dog of the larger type, but not running to fat, with that unmistakable thick, double-layer of hair. There is an outer layer of long, strong and almost wiry hair. Beneath that there is a woolly, dense undercoat. In a way, this mirrors the fowlers choice of a thornproof jacket to keep out the wind and wet, with an insulated waistcoat to keep him warm.

Many believe it is being 'cruel to be kind' to keep fowling dogs in an outside kennel, so long as it is free of draughts, whatever the weather. This enables they should stay healthy and hardy. My latest acquisition, Drake, was born in late summer and spent his first winter indoors, living as one of the family and being thoroughly 'humanised'. Then, in the spring, he was kennelled ready for serious training to start. There he will stay, at least to sleep, until he is as old as Ginny and Peat who, nowadays, prefer the fireside to the foreshore, if not the flight pond. With a joint age closer to thirty than twenty, and a long history of dusks and dawns, ducks and geese, I think they deserve it.

If a dog cannot be kennelled for whatever reason, search out a cool but draught-free spot for his basket. A dog that is used to snuggling up next to a radiator or Aga does not take kindly to the rigours of the harshest fowling conditions, and is more likely to suffer for it in later life.

A handful of spaniels — the trainer's raw material from which to fashion useful shooting companions.

CHAPTER EIGHT

Thoughts on Training

THIS BOOK WAS NEVER INTENDED AS A TRAINING MANUAL. WHY repeat what has been chronicled so many times by a stream of worthy writers? – writers who have displayed that they know how to train dogs inside out from the day when, as a pup, they are chosen from the litter, through to the day when they can be sold, or retained. What I have set out to describe in this book, however, is what comes after although, in a single volume of this size, I am more than aware that I have only been able to scratch at the surface of the mature dog's role in the shooting field.

And yet, despite my original intentions, perhaps a few words on early dog days and initial training even if only in relation to retrievers may not go amiss. If nothing else, this may help to avoid the implication that once a dog has reached a certain stage, his training is over. Most dogs are just like humans, simply because they have passed through the equivalents of primary and secondary school, initial and advanced training, does not mean that they are ready to take the world by the throat. Far from it. Wise old craftsmen shake their heads in disbelief at the blunderings of school-leaver appentices and one cannot help thinking that grey-muzzled veterans of the ten shooting seasons must react in much the same way to the antics of young dogs in their first season of work. The learning process is a continual thing and ends only with death.

Comparisons can be made between raising children and training pups. It has been said that you raise your first baby with a nappy in one hand, and a 'baby book' in the other. But by the time your second baby comes along, you may have used the one to wipe the other, having discovered that this is about all its pages are good for. Well, those may be harsh words, but they serve to introduce a few comments for those who are in the process of training their first dog with a whistle in one hand and book in the other. Read the training manual, by all means, and get the gist of what it is saying, but then set it aside, take a good long look at your dog, and let a little bit of common sense enter into the equation. That is exactly what you are going to need. Every training manual that I have come across concerns itself with a training story of what to do when things go right. Few of them tell you what to do when everything is going wrong and you are starting to wonder whether you have got the equivalent of a juvenile delinquent, or the Genghis Khan of the canine world.

TRAINING TOWARDS TARGETS

Where the 'training manual' is useful is in helping you to plan out what you will, eventually, require of your dog. For example, let us say that you are overtaken with optimism at the prospect of training your first Labrador and have started to picture how you will feel on the day that he wins his first field trial. Start out, with a pencil and paper, listing all the accomplishments that your dog will require. It will help to know on what aspects your dog will be judged, and give you targets to aim for.

On the plus side, retriever judges will look for a dog that shows natural game-finding ability, marking ability, quickness in gathering game, retrieving and delivery. They are looking for a dog with nose, drive and style, that is under control which does not need incessant and noisy handling.

On the debit side, a dog is marked down for slack and un-business-like work displayed in failing to find game, unsteadiness at heel, changing birds, disturbing ground unnecessarily and so on.

And a dog will suffer immediate elimination if it displays a hard mouth, whines or barks, runs and chases, is totally out of control or, if such a test is included, fails to enter water.

These notes, incidentally, are a summary based on the *Guide to Field Trial Judges*, issued by the Kennel Club. They are not complete, but they are enough, to give an idea of what is required.

The winning dog must display natural game-finding ability and quickness in gathering game, retrieving and delivery. It should display a 'good nose' and work with drive and style. Note that these things are either in the dog, or they are not. If they are there, they can be brought out but except in as much as the dog should have been chosen from the right stock, they cannot be implanted.

Then there are a list of 'must nots'. Some of these are measures to ensure that the wrong 'sort' will not succeed – the hard-mouthed dog, the barker and the whiner. Other dogs may be eliminated owing to a lack of basic training – dogs that are not steady, run in and chase and, generally, show that they are not under control.

This consideration of what makes a Field Trial Champion Retriever is relevant because it reveals exactly what we want from any retriever specialist, worthy of the name of working dog and shooting companion. Champion status is just the icing on a cake, in which the basic ingredient is a wet-behind-the-ears puppy.

All dogs are individuals, and have a habit of writing their own set of rules. Some puppies are sensitive little creatures who will virtually cringe at the sound of a gruff voice. Others are buffoons who need to be reminded, from time to time, that life has its serious moments. And then there are the hard cases who will exploit any signs of weakness. Such 'toughies', particularly in the case of dogs at about a year old, may seek to challenge you as 'leader of the pack', and will need to be 'sat on' hard. Each type needs a different approach.

Equally, certain fairly broad generalisations can be made that apply to virtually all pups and young dogs. One of them is that you cannot put an old head on young shoulders. Another is that if you seek to rush a young dog's education, you may ruin it completely. Such homely sayings as 'make haste slowly' in regard to dog training should, in fact, be ignored because unless you are a professional trainer, there is no need to make any sort of haste at all! Go as slowly as you like suiting your pace to the needs of your dog.

STAGES OF DEVELOPMENT

The development of children is built on firm foundations. Early days give them a sense of security within the family group. Starting at school is not just about reading and writing; it is also about learning to fit into a wider social group, and broadening horizons. The education process continues, with early, imposed discipline making way increasingly for self discipline. By now, the child is in secondary school, and developing more specialist skills and knowledge.

Things can go wrong. For example, a friend of mine was considered rather bright during his school days and, at the end of one academic year, as some sort of a reward for his achievements, he was moved up not one but two classes. Come the end of that year, he was at the bottom of his new class, and his parents were advised that he must repeat the year. Pride turned to sorrow. As the boy realised later, his repeated year did him little if any good because he never learned what had been taught to his classmates during the year that he was away from them. From that time on he would often find himself grasping the basis of a problem, but being confused as to how a solution could be reached. Teachers will, I hope, forgive me the analogy, but it was as if the boy had

144

been taught to add and subtract, then to divide, and divide again, but never to multiply. Much the same can happen with dogs.

Throw away any ideas of a training timetable. Ensure that each lesson is thoroughly learned before starting on the next, even if, after a year, your dog has progressed no further than sitting to command and walking to heel. So long as he does these two things well, you have few worries.

Having rattled on about building on the right foundations, I now have to suggest we take a few paces back. Looking again at that list of 'musts' and 'must nots'. And then at what I said about children in regard to instilled discipline as a foundation for self discipline and the eventual realisation of natural talent.

A good retriever pup should be born with the right genetic make-up to ensure that retrieving, in its broadest sense, comes naturally. The same could be said of the spaniel's in-built quartering pattern, or a pointer's inclination to point.

But what the retriever pup does *not* inherit is the knowledge that it must wait until it is given permission to retrieve, nor that it must walk to heel, and so on and so forth.

Training manuals will tell you that the basis of gundog training, especially with retrievers, is to get the dog to sit wherever and whever you want, and to stay there for as long as you want. This, other than walking closely and steadily to heel, is basically all that is required of a retriever in its initial training. To twist a saying of the Jesuits, 'Give me a puppy that will walk to heel, and sit and stay, and I will give you back a dog that should soon be ready to take its place in the shooting field.'

Novice trainers may be well advised to forget for the moment about retrieving dummies except, perhaps, to establish that the pup will at least show an interest. As to learning the basics of the three essentials, 'heel, sit and stay' you can get these, if you wish, from a gundog training manual, or a book on training the family pet. Do not despair if no specialist gundog training classes are held in your area because any dog obedience classes (perhaps run by the police) are all you require at this stage.

Having written that novice trainers may be well advised to forget about getting a young dog to retrieve dummies, I really should say something more about the subject, particularly when I have suggested that the genetic make-up of the right sort of pup should ensure that retrieving comes naturally.

I have to add that while most gundogs can develop their retrieving with a minimum of help from the trainer, with a week's experience in the shooting field being worth a year on the training paddock, we must be equally sure to guard against upsetting that natural ability.

If a puppy is keen to retrieve, do nothing to discourage it. And yes, that does mean encouragement and praise when it proudly seeks to present you with a stinkingly 'high' road casualty or a long dead rabbit, and it extends to pleading with all members of your family, if you decide against kennelling your dog, to at least try to look pleased when the pup slobbers up to them with a prized ornament, toy, intimate item of clothing, or whatever. A smack on the pup's nose at such a time is the first step on the road to ruin. You must keep the young chap thinking that he will receive nothing but praise for retrieving. It is not his fault that he cannot tell the difference between a dummy and your wife's best pair of shoes.

All that I am saying, really, is that the early days of training should not be wasted on endless, repetitive retrieves which, taken to extremes, create the risk of boring the dog. You want a keen dog. A dog that will gallop out and back with its retrieves. Repetitive dummy work is likely to produce the opposite.

The interesting equivalent of secondary school education or beyond comes next. Whatever its equivalent may be, we should not be so much seeking to instruct as to bring out the dog's natural abilities and to guide it down the right paths.

ENCOURAGING NATURAL ABILITY

Up till now, the talk has been centred on not trying to put an old head on young shoulders. We should be careful not to expect too much from the dog. From this point on, however, the emphasis shifts ever so slightly. Our concern now should be in not *under-estimating* the dog.

Throughout its early days of puppyhood and obedience training, the dog, like a young child, will have come to look upon its new owner as a source of security and comfort. In order to teach a young pup how to respond to its name and a whistle, all we have to do is call its name, run away, and it will follow. This, in fact, is how virtually all training manuals describe the process. But what some of them ignore is what can be done at a later date, when out for a walk off the lead, the dog decides to set off and explore the world on his own. Apparently deaf to our calls and whistles, he wanders off over the skyline.

Some training manuals will tell you that you should never, ever punish the dog upon his return. Up to a point, they are right. Certainly, if you are still shouting and whistling when the dog returns, then you must welcome him back, or you will confuse him entirely – chastisement suggests that he has done something wrong in returning to your call, rather than in running off. But let me offer you another scenario.

You realise, almost immediately, that the dog is wilfully ignoring your calls and whistle. The dog is telling you that he will return when *he* is good and ready. He is not totally stupid. He knows he is ignoring you. Stop whistling and calling. Wait a while and, eventually, the dog will return. And when he does, you can *see* that he knows he has done wrong and that he feels guilty. Do you rush up and tell him what a good boy he is? Might this not lead him to think that it is perfectly alright to run off, whenever he chooses?

Just stand still and do nothing. Your dog will probably stop some little distance off. Fix him with your eye, and be prepared to wait. If the dog is worth training at all, it will know that you are 'not pleased' as well as the reason why. It's a waiting game. The dog may start to crawl to you on his belly. However strong the desire to call him up, you must say nothing and let him come to you. Eventually he is up to you and, quite honestly, with a dog that is in any way sensitive, he will have suffered enough. His whole, secure world will have been toppling about him and, as I say, if he is worth training, he will know why it has happened. He will bound to heel with delight at your order. Give him your command to sit and stay, then back off twenty paces. Leave him there for a minute or so, then call him up and make a real fuss of him. Order should at least have been partially restored.

Let's now look at the more positive aspects of not under-estimating your dog, and encouraging his natural abilities.

If you have trained your dog to sit and wait while its meal is set down, then you should have no problem in getting it to sit and wait while you walk out a few paces and throw a dummy. If the dog tries to run in, despite its early training in steadiness, then you are between him and the dummy. Grab him as he passes, drag him back, and sit him down again. In either case, walk out and fetch the dummy yourself. Return to the dog, throw the dummy, and repeat the performance, collecting the dummy yourself.

On the third throw, wait a while then wave your hand forward ordering 'fetch' in an encourging tone. Your dog will immediately show you the results of generations of selective breeding as he dashes out, grabs the dummy, and retrieves it straight to you. I have found that by leaving retrieving until this stage in the dog's development his return is normally straight-forward. It is the younger, slipper-chewing dog that is more likely to skip away or try to run round you. But, if this problem does arise, any good training manual will put you right – throwing the dummy away from home, up a steep-sided lane so that he cannot easily pass you on either side, standing with your back to a wall, or simply getting down on your knees and begging. Incidentally, the only problem with young Drake, who has just reached this stage, is that he is so proud of doing that which he was born for that he will knock me over; never breaking in his galloping stride as he thrusts the dummy straight into my stomach.

Give your dog a small number of retrieves each day, always collecting two yourself for every one that you let him gather. Do this for a few days, and then stop and think. Remember what you set out to achieve. Quickness in gathering game, retrieving and delivery. You should certainly have got that, as most dogs delight in this new game. But what about marking ability, and game finding? What are you doing to develop nose, drive and style? Are you making the retrieves just a little bit too easy?

Next time out, go to an area of dense cover. Sit your dog on the edge of it. Throw the dummy high, far, and into the cover. Do not make him wait much more than about ten seconds, then send him off. On the first few attempts, he may spend an age looking for the dummy, but leave him to it. Do not under-estimate him. He is learning to use that super-sensitive nose. After a few days' practice, you should note that he is intently studying the fall of the dummy, and keeping his eye on the spot while he waits for the order to fetch. Off he goes, close to the fall, and his nose does the rest.

Next time out, throw three dummies, one after another. Gradually build up the numbers and, with them, you will be increasing your dog's marking ability, memory, and the realisation that he must go on retrieving until you tell him to stop. Think of those times when you may be asked to pick up a bird that neither you or your dog have seen fall. Leave the dog out of sight while you place a dummy. Go back and fetch him. Wave him out in your usual way. The dog will be confused, but keep waving him out, walking toward the dummy and encouraging him on. Every time that you do this, and your dog discovers the dummy, his confidence in you and himself is growing. Put out two dummies without him seeing, then three, then four.

Once the dog's confidence in these 'blind' retrieves is established, it is a simple matter to train him to signals. Remember that our field trial champion will be expected to work to signals with a minimum of fuss and to maximum effect.

Put out a 'hidden' dummy, then fetch up your dog. Sit him down, say, 10yd to the right of the dummy. Back off from him so that you are standing face-to-face and about 5yd apart. Wave your arm out toward the dummy, and take a sideways step in its direction, as you order the dog to retrieve. He should not be long in catching on. Next time, put the dummy on the other side of the dog, and repeat the performance. On the next occasion, put the dummy behind him. Take a pace toward him as you wave him back. Then place the dummy between you and call him forward as you take a pace back.

Give him experience of standing in the line. Stand close to a thick hedge or similar obstruction. An assistant, on the other side, will lob dummies over the hedge. Fire blanks at them if you wish. At the end of the proceedings, pick all the dummies, making the dog watch and, if he behaves himself, let him gather the last one. He should have marked them all.

Throw your dummies over walls and into water, and then across water. Do anything that you can think of in order to make your dummy work interesting and challenging. You will build quickly on the basic work described in the training manuals. Next time your dog is going out on a blind retrieve, replace the dummy with a cold pheasant. You should have put a few, unplucked and unhung specimens into the freezer at the end of the previous season.

In a few weeks time, you may be ready to give your dog a

taste of the real thing. Go on as before, and concentrate solidly on maintaining your dog's steadiness. Picking-up duties are perfect for adding some polish to your dog's performance, but never send him for birds that fall in plain view, or he will be encouraged to hunt with his head up rather than his nose down.

I stated earlier in this chapter that you should throw out any notions of training timetables but, because it does tend to run against the normal flow of things, let me give you just a brief idea of my own training programme, and how it affects the time at which I choose a pup. I once followed the normal course of choosing a spring-born pup. Now I look for one born in late summer, or early autumn.

Take the case of a pup born at the end of July. Such a pup is ready to move on to a new home in late September. It will live indoors throughout the winter, becoming thoroughly humanised with the family, and protected from the cold. And it makes a start on learning to respond to its name, and to sit when ordered. In spring, say at the start of May, the pup is nine months old, and ready to move into a kennel and start polishing its sitting and staying routine, and walking to heel. But there is no rush, as long as good progress has been made by August. Then come two or three months of intensive, advanced retriever training, leading up to a first introduction to the real thing in late November, which still leaves a couple of month's shooting and picking-up work.

INTRODUCTION TO THE SHOOTING FIELD

As I have stated before, this book is not intended as a training manual but, rather, a consideration of the combined role of the dog and the gun in the field. So let me leave training behind and look instead at the young dog's introduction to the shooting field. Make no mistake, these first few outings offer a truly 'make or break' set of circumstances. Temptations abound to 'do wrong' and it is up to the owner of the dog, not the calendar, to decide when his young charge is ready to face up to the real thing.

Many owners have taken out a young dog for the first time, thinking that its training days were over, only to find that it either ran wild or seemed completely ignorant of what was expected. One day the dog was getting everything right on the training paddock, and the next it was running amok in the shooting field.

If you feel you are losing control do not, whatever else might happen, try to soldier on regardless. Take the dog home or, if circumstances make this impossible, bring it to heel, put on its lead, and take the dog back to your car at the first opportunity. And do not blame the dog. He just wasn't ready. This is particularly likely to be true if you have introduced your young dog straight into a situation involving a lot of game. The transition from training ground to the shooting field should be made as gradual as possible and, if necessary, may take the whole of the dog's first season. You should not expect a dog, on his first shooting day, to sit steadily in the shooting line while twenty or more pheasants rain down about him.

This takes us back to the point about a dog's training extending throughout his days in the shooting field. A process that may continue through till death. No-one would expect a novice shot, having only had one or two lessons at the shooting school, to put a good performance at, say, grouse hustling downwind over a short skyline on the moor. Neither should they think that they can 'throw a dog in at the deep end' and expect it to perform creditably.

The rabbit, duck and pigeon are the gundog trainer's likeliest best options for introducing a young dog to the real thing. Shoot a rabbit or two in the late summer over your spaniel, or in front of your heel-keeping Labrador. Then take him home. Next time out, if all has gone well, you might shoot two or three, then three or four.

In September there are few better experiences for a retriever than to wait patiently at a flight pond. Again, you will just shoot two or three duck on these outings and, if you want to ingrain those lessons in steadiness, you will strive to drop your ducks on land rather than water. That way, you can leave your dog on the drop and gather them yourself. The dog is realising that he does not necessarily retrieve everything that falls. Next time out, you can give him one retrieve, and then two, and so on. Whether you regard this as training or shooting does not matter, so long as you keep steering the dog in the right direction.

And all the time you are building your dog's experience of the sport. He is learning what he can and cannot do. If I can be excused an outrageous misquote, he is deivered from evil, and not led into temptation.

153

Hit or miss at a wide, crossing pheasant. Note the footwork.

154

CHAPTER NINE

Random Shots

THROUGHOUT THE PAGES OF THIS BOOK, I HAVE BEEN CONCEN-
trating, very largely, upon what we can expect from our gundogs.
It might be as well, in this chapter, to consider what they might
expect from us!

Oh, I am not thinking about feeding, kennelling and
veterinary care. All that has been covered in detail in a number
of excellent books. No, what I am talking about is the occasion
when you miss a simple, going-away shot at a driven grouse, and
an Irish setter fixes its eye on you as much as to say 'Is that the
best you can do?'

Or it might be the harshest of harsh dawns when you and
your Labrador have been waiting for hours and you know that
you have just missed the only chance you are likely to get of a
goose. Up swing those liquid, brown eyes, 'Is that what you
dragged me out for?'

And it might be a time when you are watching a wily old
cock pheasant, cackling insults back over its shoulder, as it skims
away down some fenland hedge. As you break your gun and
smell the cordite, up pops your little spaniel, 'Is that what I've
been busting a gut for, this last half hour?'

If you have not experienced these things, then you must be
either an excellent shot, or very lucky in your choice of
diplomatic dogs. Not that I mind their looks because I appreciate
what the dogs may be feeling, something like the rugby forward
who has worked long and hard to win the ball, only to see it

155

dropped by the backs.

And so, let us turn the tables on ourselves and take a few random shots at suggesting what dogs would like to see from their owners. It might be summed up as 'good shooting'.

GOOD SHOOTING

What constitutes good shooting? I know it when I see it, and yet I am still in the dark as to how it is achieved. Are good shots born or made? Hopefully, we may all improve with practice.

Practice would give us sound judgement and efficient footwork, often described as the foundations of good shooting. Sound judgement means not only the automatic ability to judge the speed and range of a target, but also the best time and place to shoot it. Good shooters instinctively know to take an approaching bird when it is still well in front, or to snap off a shot at the snipe that rises into the wind. The feet come into that as well, because we should be getting them into their best position to give the body, arms and guns the freedom to move and swing, without conscious thought. Good shots give the impression of having all the time in the world and it is only when you try to get off a shot before them that you realise how quick they truly are; virtually shooting by instinct.

What is to be made of a statement such as 'old-so-and-so is a good shot'? I only ask because the 1990, Game Fair issue of *Shooting Times* included a series of interviews with men described as the 'First Eleven of Game Shooters'. I do not doubt that they are all exceptionally good shots, but in what circumstances? Have their names become legends simply upon their abilities to shoot driven pheasants and grouse? Could they roll over eight rabbits out of ten? The best snipe shot that I know cannot, almost literally, hit any other target. But his footwork on the bog is a marvel. We call him 'The Frog'. He seems able to skip from tussock to tussock and is never caught wrong-footed while others flounder as a snipe 'scaaps', 'zigs' and 'zags'. The man who can stand outside a covet and kill high, curling pheasants with the best of them may not necessarily look so clever on the steep, heather banks of a walked-up grouse moor.

Perhaps good shooting, in its widest sense, should be seen as the ability to cope successfully, in any given set of conditions, and with any kind of quarry, rather than any sort of specialist skill. One important aspect of this is the ability to estimate range with a fair degree of accuracy.

GUESSTIMATING RANGE

Introduce the subject of estimating killing range into a shooting conversation and most folk automatically think of men they know who habitually shoot at birds that are obviously out of range. Geese crossing the shore are an obvious example.

There is another side to the coin. How many birds owe their lives to cautious folk who, quite honestly, do not have the faintest idea of what is a maximum but killable range? This is often seen when out shooting over spaniels or pointers. A bird gets up at extreme range, not to be saluted. An obvious example is the snipe that flushes well out, ahead of the guns. It looks tiny at 40yd, but is well within range of a load of 8 shot from a barrel with some degree of choke.

Of course, it is always better to err on the side of caution. To fire at birds when they are out of range not only makes them ever wilder and unapproachable, but it can also lead to unnecessary suffering when birds are pricked. At the same time, it is surely folly to be so unaware of distances that birds within deadly range are regularly allowed to go. I remember being congratulated on a Cornish woodcock shoot for having pulled down a long shot. The bird had certainly been wide but it was not, I thought, all that far. I paced it out. Just under 35yd and well within shot. But my friend was quite ecstatic.

It pays, I find, to have some clearly definable distance in mind; something you know intimately; against which to judge range. In my case, it is the length of a cricket pitch, which is 22yd. If I judge a bird to be within two cricket pitch lengths of my position, then I fire. If I am in any doubt, I let it pass.

Vertical range is far harder to judge. Men will regularly judge high flying pheasants to be out of range when they are 90ft, 30yd up. Look at a modern, nine-storey office block. At about 90ft high, compare the scale of a pigeon flying on a level with the roof, knowing that each storey of a modern building will be about 10ft, we can study a variety of buildings, and apply what we have learned in the shooting field.

STAMINA

It was stated of woodcock and snipe, that a sportsman could not make the most of the bog-trotting style of sport unless he was reasonable fit. This fitness, and stamina, helps toward making a good bag in two ways. Firstly, and most obviously, it is virtually impossible to hold a gun straight when your chest is heaving and your heart drumming wildly. Secondly, the fit shooter is capable of walking for longer, and further. The greater the amount of ground that is covered, then the greater the bag is likely to be. The strain of shooting a hundred or more cartridges on a driven shoot creates different physical strains, but strains nevertheless. Unless a man keeps reasonably fit, he cannot get the best out of shooting in any of its styles. Many of the best shooters who I have known have kept themselves in first-class physical condition. No tobacco, a modest amount of alcohol, early hours, regular exercise. Miserable beggars, but they shot straight!

TACTICS AND AWARENESS

What some of us lack in stamina, we may hope to make up for in the application of considered tactics. Such tactics can be difficult to apply in the formal field of driven shooting, where you must act as part of a team. But there is little to stop you adopting a few clever little tactics when shooting alone or in a small party. For example, most right-handed shooters find they do better on crossing shots that approach from their right, and will arrange themselves accordingly when, say, choosing a side on which to flank a pointing setter. When walking behind a spaniel, he will be keeping an eye on the dog. If he sees its tail accelerating and its interest heightening, he will be easing himself into position for the coming shot long before the spaniel flushes the squatting bird.

In many shooting situations, it puts you at a great advantage to have the ability to think and act in the blinking of an eye. For example, the securing of a coveted right-and-left at woodcock has, on those occasions that I have witnessed it, depended rather more in taking a quick decision than on particularly straight shooting. We talk of shooters having a 'good eye' in the same way that a skilled horseman has 'good hands'. This is, again, not necessarily so much concerned with aiming accuracy as the ability to sum up a situation that presents itself in a fraction of a second.

Think again of the example of the woodcock. Say that two birds had flushed in the same instant, one at 15yd and the other at 35yd. The man whose eye is instinctively drawn to the closer bird may find, if he shoots it first, that the other bird has passed out of range before he can get off a second shot. If he had dealt with the more distant one first, he should have had plenty of time to finish with the closer bird. But it may have been that the closer bird was just about to flit back into the covert, while the further bird was flying into clear space . . .

WHEN WE MISS

If we take all the opportunities with which we are presented, standing or walking, whatever and whenever, most of us will have to accept that we will miss at least as much as we hit. This is inevitable and, if it were otherwise, if we picked only our favourite angles for example, the whole thing would be more of an execution than a sport. But that does not stop us knowing which shot suits us best, and which the least.

Pheasant, but also ducks and pigeons, can cause us all problems when they are flying high, dipping and curling. Who can claim consistently to hit the high pheasant, gliding away behind the line, or the low, swerving grouse that has passed through the butts? At least the pheasant looks spectacular, whereas the grouse, despite all its problems, might appear quite mundane. The list goes on.

But how can we explain these and other misses to our dogs. Should they be interested in our excuses and explanations. We say that to err is human, but does that explain why, when the tables are turned, so many of us refuse to make allowances for our dogs? If we accept them, as I think we should, as shooting companions rather than servants, as characters and individuals rather than automated game getters and gatherers, then will we not forgive them their faults? So what if your setter 'blinked' a woodcock, if you missed the last one? If your Labrador fails on a runner, ask why it was a runner in the first place, and what if your spaniel breaks his bounds occasionally. Next time you swear at your dog for taking a step toward a bird that falls close to the line of guns, think only that he may have done it out of surprise at your scoring a hit. To err is human, certainly. Should it be only a canine trait to forgive?